Let God Be True
A father's journey continues

By Cesar Torres

Copyright © 2020, Cesar Torres

ISBN: 13: 978-1-7328615-6-5

Let God Be True
A father's journey continues

Cesar Torres

Table of Contents

Romans 3:4

Certainly not! Indeed, **let God be true** but every man a liar. As it is written: "That You may be justified in Your words, And may overcome when You are judged."

Introduction - The Truth Comes from God

It has been nearly three years, since I self-published a book on Amazon, dealing with my journey into new territory as my daughter moved into a same sex relationship. In that book, I spoke about my reaction to this change as well as a desire to reach the Christian community on the confusion around this topic. There is a lot of deception that has taken place regarding this sin as we have succumbed to the modern day thinking, and acceptance, of this lifestyle.

My thoughts while writing the first book was that I would create a blog, or website, to continue to address the issue, but after several negative comments, and feedback, by those I love, I took a step back to reflect. I should have been better prepared for some of the negative, sometimes brutal comments, but no matter how well prepared you think you are, it's always difficult to hear accusations that you are unloving, uncaring, and self-righteous.

So, after much reflection on what had occurred, and the Lord's guidance, I've determined to complete the task, that I feel, I've been assigned. This book is a result of the Lord's continued prompting, and I pray that the Lord will give me the strength, and the wisdom to deal with the attacks to come. I'm not fearful for myself, but do realize there are others I must consider when I take on the risks of bucking the current wave of the culture. I'm now ready to engage in the spiritual battle of this age, and speak God's truth according to His word.

I'm not doing this for my sake, but for the sake of those that have been deceived, in a culture that accepts same sex relationships as normal. God's word, the Bible, is still the ultimate authority on human sexuality, and nothing can, or will, change that. Ultimately, there are lives, and souls, at stake in this battle and we need to be engaged in sounding the alarm, and ensuring we have done all we can to warn, not only those we love, but also anyone that is in jeopardy.

Make no mistake about it, there is a battle raging, but we can no longer stay silent as a community of believers. Yet the battle will not be fought with the weapons of this culture, or on the same battlefield, that we have been pulled into in the past.

The apostle Paul in the book of Ephesians tells us to put on the armor of God in order to make our stand against the devil. He describes the forces, and powers, we'll face, and then all the components of God's armor, we will need in this battle. He describes the function of each piece of the armor, and how we are to use it in this battle. Each piece of the armor plays a role, and they work together for us in order to stand for His word, and deliver the truth to make known the mystery of the gospel, and salvation in Jesus Christ.

Ephesians 6:11-20
[11] Put on the whole armor of God, that you may be able to stand against the wiles of the devil. [12] For we

do not wrestle against flesh and blood, but against principalities, against powers, against the rulers of the darkness of this age, against spiritual *hosts* of wickedness in the heavenly *places.* [13] Therefore take up the whole armor of God, that you may be able to withstand in the evil day, and having done all, to stand.

[14] Stand therefore, having girded your waist with truth, having put on the breastplate of righteousness, [15] and having shod your feet with the preparation of the gospel of peace; [16] above all, taking the shield of faith with which you will be able to quench all the fiery darts of the wicked one. [17] And take the helmet of salvation, and the sword of the Spirit, which is the word of God; [18] praying always with all prayer and supplication in the Spirit, being watchful to this end with all perseverance and supplication for all the saints— [19] and for me, that utterance may be given to me, that I may open my mouth boldly to make known the mystery of the gospel, [20] for which I am an ambassador in chains; that in it I may speak boldly, as I ought to speak.

At the end of the above scripture we see that the apostle Paul also needed, and asked, for prayer that he may open his mouth boldly to share the gospel. I've had to figure out how to share the gospel, and have realized that my way has been through my writing. I'm not eloquent of speech, and have a deep fear of public speaking. So, I'll try to be bold in this way, and pray that when faced with opposition, that the Lord will give me the words to speak boldly.

My intent is not to be offensive in this battle, or use language that is divisive, argumentative, or insensitive, but I'm sure to some extent I will be all of the above. I'll also be unapologetic about my stand on God's word, and the authority of His word, the Bible. Scripture is clear that God created man and woman, male and female, in His image.

It's also clear that God called same sex relationships sin, and that a same sex marriage doesn't really exist in the Lord's world, so those who want to call it marriage, go right ahead. It is still sin, with a new name, or label, as defined by a culture that rejects God. Sin can't be hidden from God and denying it, and railing against it, won't make that fact go away.

As I go through this, I'll write a brief chapter on, what I believe are three common delusions, as well as some of the most common issues, excuses and justification for this particular sin. I will give my own personal thoughts, but base them on God's word. I'll also share my own testimony to clarify what the Lord has done in my life, and show that the Lord is able to do much with any sinner, who comes to Him with a repentant, contrite spirit, and a willing heart. Some of my topics will be taken from discussions, headlines, or arguments from across multiple mediums such as the web, television, radio, etc., but ultimately referring people back to God's word.

My primary goal is to call the Christian church back to God's word on this issue. My secondary goal is to reach out to Christian's that have, or are going through, something similar. I've heard from some parents that are experiencing difficult times because their children have turned to same sex relationships.

In addition, there are few outlets for Christian parents, or relatives, that are hurting for their loved one, to reach out to, or discuss this issue. Since the culture now considers this decision a birthright, instead of a choice, it has been normalized, and there is an insensitivity, to put it mildly, towards Christians, due to the acceptance of this lifestyle.

You may have noticed I've stayed away from using the common phrases used to describe same sex relationships in our culture, and that is intentional. If you had a chance to read my first book, *"Mom, Dad, I'm Gay, A father's journey,"* you would understand. I'm not going to be called bigoted, or hateful, for using labels that people have placed on themselves. I will describe sin as the Lord described it, and make my case, as I feel the Lord is leading me to present it.

I've taken God's word for the title of this book. The capital letters, LGBT, are emphasized to stand for, "Let God Be True" taken from Romans 3, but when you look at the verse in your Bible, please notice the second half of the verse, "but every man a liar." It's so clear when looking at this verse that we are all sinners, and liars, only God is true to His word and promises. However, with society wanting to eliminate God from our daily lives, it's no wonder we have gone so far in accepting sin, sinful lives, and behavior that contradicts His word.

My hope, and prayer, is that my journey will be beneficial to all that take it with me. I perceive that we need to address a culture that needs us, the true Christian church, to stand in the gap for those that are perishing, and the salvation that only Jesus Christ can offer.

Jesus has the truth and is the truth. In the meantime, we are flawed. At best we are liars, at worse deceitful, as well as cunning and evil. In the book of John, Jesus made it clear that there is only one way to God, the Father, and that is through Him.

John 14:6
Jesus said to him, "I am the way, the truth, and the life. No one comes to the Father except through Me."

In the verse above, Jesus also declared Himself to be "the truth." Many have forsaken truth in order to justify themselves, and live within a society that only wants to hear things which allows them to live the way they want to live.

Anything that restricts, accuses, or makes a person feel bad about their choices are condemned. People are living their lives with blinders on, they hear without comprehension, and are without understanding. They deny that there are consequences for their sin.

They don't acknowledge that the consequences of sin are separation from God, and ultimately judgment, which will result in their eternal separation from the Lord.

There are those today that refuse God's word, they not only make a choice to do so, but they deceive others, and twist the truth. These can only be called one thing, and that is evil, and the Lord states that many times throughout His word. In the book of Romans, we read the following:

<u>Romans 3:10-18</u>
"There is none righteous, no, not one;
[11] There is none who understands;
There is none who seeks after God.
[12] They have all turned aside;
They have together become unprofitable;
There is none who does good, no, not one."
[13] "Their throat *is* an open tomb;
With their tongues they have practiced deceit";
"The poison of asps *is* under their lips";
[14] "Whose mouth *is* full of cursing and bitterness."
[15] "Their feet *are* swift to shed blood;
[16] Destruction and misery *are* in their ways;
[17] And the way of peace they have not known."
[18] "There is no fear of God before their eyes."

Please note the following from Psalm 111.

<u>Psalm 111:10</u>
The fear of the Lord *is* the beginning of wisdom; A good understanding have all those who do *His commandments.* His praise endures forever.

When looking at the Old and New Testaments we clearly see the reason why we see a society full of deceit and evil, "There is no fear of God." Those who fear the Lord gain wisdom, and a good understanding, to follow His commandments. Since God has been removed from people's lives and society, we are seeing the results of a society that places their own wisdom, and understanding, above God's word.

In Romans 3 above, the Apostle Paul compiled a list of Old Testament passages from the book of Psalms and Proverbs to stress human sinfulness, our depravity, and eventual destruction without God. The "fear" of God in these verses is about having the proper attitude of God, and a devout reverence for Him. The absence of that proper attitude leads people astray into sin and depravity.

As we think through God's word, and our ways, there is a scripture verse that best describes our current culture, and the thoughts that occupy a person's heart and mind.

Proverbs 14:12
There is a way *that seems* right to a man,
But its end *is* the way of death.

Looking at that verse, I know there have been times in my own life, where I thought something seemed right for me. Even as a professing Christian, I've made choices, decisions, set a course, or direction, that seemed right. In some cases, I've made some good choices and decisions, but there have been some really bad ones as well that were unfruitful, or outright wrong.

Our lives are full of those moments, and most of us don't consult anyone, let alone the Lord. Rejecting God, and the truth of His word, leads to death, but it's not an instantaneous physical death, and ultimately the death referred to here is hell. Eternal separation from God.

I'm seeing a growing trend that those who disagree with a Christian worldview are intolerant, and verbally abusive of those of faith, yet we are the ones that are labeled, or called, bigoted, or hateful. I truly don't understand how, and when, we got to the point, where someone's faith is considered hateful or bigoted. Hate comes from an evil heart not a faithful heart.

Isaiah 5:20
Woe to those who call evil good, and good evil; Who put darkness for light, and light for darkness; Who put bitter for sweet, and sweet for bitter!

The prophet Isaiah warned the people of his day because they were twisting what was good and calling evil good. This is exactly what we see today. People are calling sin good, and labeling those that expose it as evil.

Luke 6:45
A good man out of the good treasure of his heart brings forth good; and an evil man out of the evil treasure of his heart brings forth evil. For out of the abundance of the heart his mouth speaks.

It is interesting to see, and hear, some of the words that come out of the mouths of those that oppose Christianity. Often their mouths are filled with profanity, and cursing, and that to me speaks to the condition of their heart.

Matthew 15:18
But those things which proceed out of the mouth come from the heart, and they defile a man.

The evil that the Christian is accused off, comes out of the mouths of those that accuse, and attack us, from what is in their hearts. The heart of the Christian is to reach the lost, give them the gospel, the good news of salvation through Jesus Christ. To not give someone the truth of salvation would be evil because people's souls are at stake.

John 3:16-18
[16] For God so loved the world that He gave His only begotten Son, that whoever believes in Him should not perish but have everlasting life. [17] For God did not send His Son into the world to condemn the world, but that the world through Him might be saved.
[18] "He who believes in Him is not condemned; but he who does not believe is condemned already, because he has not believed in the name of the only begotten Son of God.

Psalm 25:5
Lead me in Your truth and teach me,
For You *are* the God of my salvation;
On You I wait all the day.

If only our accusers would allow their hearts to listen to the words, we give them. Those words would bring life to their souls, and lead them to the salvation offered by Jesus Christ. Instead, they condemn, accuse us, and shut their ears, while attacking with such viciousness at times, that they shut out the Holy Spirit from working in their lives. All we can do at that point is pray for them, and realize that we are also sinners, saved by grace, by a God who doesn't wish for anyone to perish.

2 Peter 3:9
The Lord is not slack concerning *His* promise, as some count slackness, but is longsuffering toward us, not willing that any should perish but that all should come to repentance.

So, what does the Bible tell us about truth? There are many references to what is true in scripture, and the word truth is used often to describe God's word, His work, His righteousness, His justice, and His sanctification.

Psalm 33:4
For the word of the Lord *is* right,
And all His work *is done* in truth.

Psalm 119:160
The entirety of Your word *is* truth,
And every one of Your righteous judgments *endures* forever.

Deuteronomy 32:4
He is the Rock, His work *is* perfect;
For all His ways *are* justice,

A God of truth and without injustice;
Righteous and upright *is* He.

John 17:17
[17] Sanctify them by Your truth. Your word is truth.

In the scripture above, Jesus prayed to God that His disciples would be sanctified by the truth, God's word. Sanctification is defined in the dictionary, as being set apart to a sacred purpose, or religious use, as well as to free from sin. Jesus understood that his disciples would need God's truth to be able to deliver the message of salvation He had given them.

The Christian church needs to be sanctified with the truth of God's word, in this day, and during this age, where truth is challenged. I'm reminded of the words Pontius Pilate said to Jesus as he questioned Him in his court.

John 18:38
Pilate said to Him, "What is truth?" And when he had said this, he went out again to the Jews, and said to them, "I find no fault in Him at all."

It's interesting to note that Pilate questioned truth, and yet clearly stated he found no fault in Jesus. I find that ironic since he did know the truth, that there was nothing Jesus had done to stand before him, accused of misleading the people, and other ambiguous crimes. The accusations that were bought to Pilate were at best lies, but were in truth, evil fabrications.

Proverbs 14:25
A true witness delivers souls,
But a deceitful *witness* speaks lies.

Looking at the next couple of verses, from the scriptures above in the book of John, we get a glimpse of the accusations made, of Jesus' crimes. They were ambiguous at best, but truly were just lies made by evil men, that were seeking His destruction, and eventually His death.

John 18:29-30
[29] Pilate then went out to them and said, "What accusation do you bring against this Man?"
[30] They answered and said to him, "If He were not an evildoer, we would not have delivered Him up to you."

In the gospels of Matthew chapter 27, Mark chapter 15, and Luke 23, we are given a little more information, on the accusations made against Jesus, which were primarily around misleading the people.

Matthew 27:13-14
[13] Then Pilate said to Him, "Do You not hear how many things they testify against You?" [14] But He answered him not one word, so that the governor marveled greatly.

Mark 15:3-4
[3] And the chief priests accused Him of many things, but He answered nothing. [4] Then Pilate asked Him again, saying, "Do You answer nothing? See how many things they testify against You!"

Luke 23:13-14

[13] Then Pilate, when he had called together the chief priests, the rulers, and the people, [14] said to them, "You have brought this Man to me, as one who misleads the people.

In both the gospels of Matthew and Mark, we find that Pilate knew the truth, the reason for the accusations against Jesus, and why He was presented to him for judgement and crucifixion.

Matthew 27:18

"For he knew that they had handed Him over because of envy."

Mark 15:10

[10] For he knew that the chief priests had handed Him over because of envy.

Simply put they **envied** Jesus.

Proverbs 14:30

A sound heart *is* life to the body,
But envy *is* rottenness to the bones.

Yet, knowing the truth, the reason for their accusations, didn't stop Pilate from doing the wrong thing. The truth didn't deter Pilate back then, and today the truth doesn't deter many who want their way, or are listening to others, and being led astray by lies and deceit.

They profess to know the truth, or like Pilate ask, "What is truth? The reality is that they don't care about the truth because they are self-seeking. Confusion clouds the minds of those seeking their own gratification, and their own ways, and therefore evil is present there.

James 3:16
For where envy and self-seeking *exist,* confusion and every evil thing *are* there.

There are times like this when I'm feeling that I'm being a little preachy. My intent is not to preach since I'm not a preacher, or to lay a heavy burden on anyone. I'm basically a man with a desire to call people back to God, for only one very simple reason, for the salvation of those around us, and to be ambassadors of Christ, to a dying culture.

Please, I beg of you, if you don't know the truth of God's word seek it and find it, not for my sake, but for yours. Jesus stated that there will be those that essentially will miss the boat, and not enter into the kingdom of heaven.

Matthew 7:21-23
[21] "Not everyone who says to Me, 'Lord, Lord,' shall enter the kingdom of heaven, but he who does the will of My Father in heaven. [22] Many will say to Me in that day, 'Lord, Lord, have we not prophesied in Your name, cast out demons in Your name, and done many wonders in Your name?' [23] And then I will declare to them, 'I never knew you; depart from Me, you who practice lawlessness!'

If you are not doing God's will, and speaking His truth, the Lord may refuse you entry into his kingdom. May the Lord bless you in your search for His truth, not man's truth.

1 John 1:9

If we confess our sins, He is faithful and just to forgive us *our* sins and to cleanse us from all unrighteousness.

My Testimony - A Sinner

As I mentioned I've had to deal with some criticism after making my stand on my daughter's lifestyle, and it got worse after I wrote my first book. I don't mention it to get sympathy because to be honest I can be pretty pig headed, and sometimes insensitive. I mention it to show that standing up for God's word in our current culture does require us to be prepared.

It's not just about being prepared for the criticism, but as I mentioned previously, there is a spiritual battle that comes along as part of it. The criticism and attacks seem to be targeted at you, but ultimately, it's an attack on our Lord, and we must recognize it's a spiritual battle we're engaged in, and the goal is to save souls.

So why provide my testimony, my story? I'm no different than most men, but I thought it necessary to give you my background so you'll understand where I'm coming from, and that I'm not here to judge, or make accusations. Ultimately, the Lord is the judge and we'll all stand before Him. I was, and still am, a sinner that was fortunate to find the Lord, and blessed beyond my own merits. I only found God because one day I determined to seek, and find Him, no other reason.

It didn't happen overnight and it didn't take place because I deserved it, but because God is merciful and graceful. So, my testimony, about how I came to my faith in Jesus Christ, is the reason that I must speak of God's plan of salvation for all mankind, and not just mine.

Deuteronomy 4:29
But from there you will seek the Lord your God, and you will find *Him* if you seek Him with all your heart and with all your soul

Jeremiah 29:13
And you will seek Me and find *Me,* when you search for Me with all your heart.

Matthew 7:7-8
[7] "Ask, and it will be given to you; seek, and you will find; knock, and it will be opened to you. [8] For everyone who asks receives, and he who seeks finds, and to him who knocks it will be opened.

I was raised in New York City, living most of my young life in Brooklyn, in a "Catholic" home. I don't intend to slam Catholics, or their faith, but if you had asked me about my beliefs, or religion, I would have stated I was a Catholic, and believed in God. That was the extent of what I understood of religion, or God. I simply knew He existed, and He was the creator of all things.

My parents didn't attend church regularly, but would go for Easter, and sometimes Christmas. I don't ever remember hearing anything that made me believe in the need for salvation, or that Jesus Christ died for my sins. There was a lot of kneeling and standing in church, a priest read from the Bible, people took something in their mouths, and drank from a cup, but there was no connection to anything for me. My parents never explained anything to us about our faith, or what they believed, and while I'm sure that's not everyone's experience that's how I remember it.

As a young person growing up in Brooklyn during the 60's and 70's, I really thought I would die young. I wasn't ever afraid of dying, and for the most part, I felt I was good enough to go to heaven, if I should die. Once I grew up and left home, I felt I was a moral, and good person, knowing right from wrong.

I was fortunate enough, blessed really, but I didn't know it at the time, to get into a good college, and made an effort to make a better life for myself. I married young, being "in love," but unfortunately divorced five years later. Looking back now I can see that I was selfish, and left my wife, and my beautiful daughter to seek freedom.

Freedom from what, to this day I don't know, and couldn't explain it if I tried. My reasoning, or excuse, was that I was no longer "in love." But thinking on that today, and my different frame of mind, what did that really mean? Yep, I was just selfish.

We throw that word "love" around a lot to describe how we feel. We'll say things that describe emotions, such as how my heart no longer belongs to that person, or I deserve to be happy. We'll go on using other terms such as we're no longer soul mates. What it boils down to is that my excuses were as lame then, as they are today, when I hear them from others. What it all boiled down to was that I wanted to experience something else in life that appealed to me more than what I had, or believed that I needed, or deserved.

Scripture tells us in **Jeremiah 17:9**
"The heart *is* deceitful above all *things,* And desperately wicked; Who can know it?

I was relying on my feelings, emotions, and/or my heart, and was deceived to what was true and real. My ex-wife loved me, and I let her down because I was only thinking about my wants, and my needs. Selfish man that I was, and for the most part still am, I didn't care about the hurt I was causing others.

There are things that scripture tells us, that come, or proceed, from our hearts.

Matthew 15:19
For out of the heart proceed evil thoughts, murders, adulteries, fornications, thefts, false witness, blasphemies.

Our hearts are not pure because we are not born pure. The Bible tells us we are born sinners, and it goes back to the beginning, the first book of the Bible, Genesis, where God created all things. God created man and woman on the sixth day of creation, but man sinned against God, and was cursed for his disobedience. Since then we have all inherited a sinful nature, and are in need of a savior, and that's where Jesus Christ comes in.

It's interesting as I think about Adam and Eve. Here were two human beings, they were created in the image of God, just met, had no other person to choose from, weren't given any other option, or choice, for the most part this was the first arranged marriage, yet God instructed them to be fruitful and multiply.

Genesis 1:22
And God blessed them, saying, "Be fruitful and multiply, and fill the waters in the seas, and let birds multiply on the earth."

Isn't that interesting that they could not complain about being incompatible, or that the other wasn't attractive enough, or the other person doesn't make me feel valued. I could go on and on with the many excuses, and reasons, given for divorce and separation. I know, I used some of them myself, and almost did a second time, when at one point I wanted out of my second marriage.

The difference the second time around was that there was much more at stake. I had two more kids, and my wife had also been through a divorce. We had agreed, when we first discussed marriage that we would not even mention the word divorce, unless we were both sure it was the only recourse. So, we struggled along and as we did, many things occurred in my work life, and career, where I hit that proverbial "brick wall."

I lost my job due to poor judgment, to put it mildly, and found myself adrift without a job, career, and fearful that I couldn't find something else to provide for my family. I knew I'd made some very bad choices, and mistakes, but my wife stood by me. Although I'm sure she was angry about the situation I'd put us in, she didn't point out how stupid I'd been, or remind me how bad things were, but comforted me, and assured me we would get through it.

At this point in my life, I wanted to crawl into a corner, shrivel up, and die. However, it's never that simple, so each day I got up, and did my best to find a job, and any work that would help to provide for us. At that time, I also made a promise in desperation to God. I would go to church every day for a year, and pray for God to forgive me, or at least give me peace, and to help me.

Looking back, it may seem like a foolish promise, but I was determined to keep it. So, I started going to the only church I knew, the Catholic church. I would go into any nearby church, while I looked for work, or when I found miscellaneous, and/or temporary work.

Any local Catholic church would do. All I did was go in, sit, or stand somewhere, say a silent prayer and leave. I never stayed to hear a priest or service, never went to confession. I had never felt comfortable telling, or confessing, to a stranger my faults and failings, except now as part of the testimony of my salvation.

There were many days where I couldn't find a local church while I traveled looking for work, or during the day, to and from temporary work. In those instances when I'd get back home, I would drive to the local church in our town. Many evenings, after 11 pm, although the church was closed, I would go to a small area in the front of the church, and say a quick prayer and leave.

My routine lasted for a little over a year, and my situation wasn't drastically improved. I was still without a permanent job, sometimes fearful, and usually worried, but I felt I had kept my promise to God, and that gave me some comfort.

Soon after completing my promise, my wife and I were invited to a local neighbor's home. They were having a "get together" with some friends, and invited us to join them. By now I'm sure by my name you know I'm Hispanic, but more accurately of Puerto Rican heritage. In those days, and maybe still true today, when you invite a Puerto Rican to a "get together," that would usually be interpreted as a party.

We purchased a bottle of liquor to take to this "get together," and when we arrived our hostess smiled, took the bottle, and placed it on the back of her kitchen counter. She then led us into her home and introduced us to her friends.

As we began to speak with people, we realized this was not what we would call a party. You may have guessed it by now, but we were attending a "home fellowship," that our neighbors were having with members of their local church. It was very pleasant, and we had a nice time, but there was one person that was determined to find out just one thing. "If we were to die today, did we know whether we were going to heaven or hell?"

Her name was Edna, and she was determined to know where we stood with God. She would go back and forth in the house, speaking to my wife, and then to me, and neither one of us would give her a straight answer. She finally got us together, and when we would not give her a straight answer, she invited us to her church for the following day.

To pacify her, we agreed to go to the church, and at the time we hadn't realized how that decision would change our lives. Our visit to the church was the beginning of a change, and transformation, in our lives that has carried forward into everything we do, and believe.

That Sunday we attended an Assemblies of God, denominational church. I can't say I remember the sermon, but that day I realized there was a God, and that He loved me, and that I could repent of my sin, and He would forgive me. All I had to do was repent and follow Him, and that His name was Jesus.

I'm sure that may sound simplistic but when I left church that day, I made some immediate changes in my life. I hadn't really ever read the Bible, although I had looked inside of it, and read some paragraphs, or verses. Yet when I got home, I knew there was something I needed to do, which was to get rid of all idols I had in the house.

Up to that point in my life I had never read about, or understood idolatry, or a belief in false gods. The sermon, although I don't remember it, wasn't about idols, yet something drove me that day to clear out a bunch of figurines of so-called saints that I had in my home. You see at that time I had been into "spiritualism," which at the time I thought was driven by my desire to find God.

For the most part spiritualism is based on believing in so called saints, praying to them, and communicating with the dead. Usually you are led, or instructed by a "medium," that claims to speak to the dead, and speaks to us on their behalf, warning and guiding us. In reality, the Lord showed me, before I had even read it in scripture, that this was a form of idolatry and witchcraft.

As I started to read and learn from the word of God, I realized that God is jealous for us. Not the kind of jealousy we understand as earthly beings, but that He wants and desires the best for us, and for that to occur, He wants us to be faithful to Him, and put Him first in our lives. As I read the Ten Commandments, it became clear to me that I was sinful and needed to repent before God.

Exodus 20:1-17
And God spoke all these words, saying:

[2] "I *am* the LORD your God, who brought you out of the land of Egypt, out of the house of bondage.
[3] "You shall have no other gods before Me.
[4] "You shall not make for yourself a carved image— any likeness *of anything* that *is* in heaven above, or

that *is* in the earth beneath, or that *is* in the water under the earth; ⁵ you shall not bow down to them nor [b]serve them. For I, the LORD your God, *am* a jealous God, visiting the iniquity of the fathers upon the children to the third and fourth *generations* of those who hate Me, ⁶ but showing mercy to thousands, to those who love Me and keep My commandments.

⁷ "You shall not take the name of the LORD your God in vain, for the LORD will not hold *him* guiltless who takes His name in vain.

⁸ "Remember the Sabbath day, to keep it holy. ⁹ Six days you shall labor and do all your work, ¹⁰ but the seventh day *is* the Sabbath of the LORD your God. *In it* you shall do no work: you, nor your son, nor your daughter, nor your male servant, nor your female servant, nor your cattle, nor your stranger who *is* within your gates. ¹¹ For *in* six days the LORD made the heavens and the earth, the sea, and all that *is* in them, and rested the seventh day. Therefore the LORD blessed the Sabbath day and hallowed it.

¹² "Honor your father and your mother, that your days may be long upon the land which the LORD your God is giving you.

¹³ "You shall not murder.

¹⁴ "You shall not commit adultery.

¹⁵ "You shall not steal.

¹⁶ "You shall not bear false witness against your neighbor.

¹⁷ "You shall not covet your neighbor's house; you shall not covet your neighbor's wife, nor his male

servant, nor his female servant, nor his ox, nor his donkey, nor anything that *is* your neighbor's."

As I had grown into an adult, I had added idols and gods into my life, such as the carved (clay) images of saints I prayed to. I took God's name in vain, and never cared, or understood why anyone would dedicate a day to worship God. My parents were a mess, and divorced, how could I honor them when they made a mess of their lives, and I sometimes blamed them for the mess I'd made of my own life.

Adultery, I had been married, and divorced, so once I remarried, I was considered an adulterer. In addition, Jesus states that if a man looks at another woman in lust, he has committed adultery in his heart. How many times had I been guilty of that sin?

I had taken things that didn't belong to me, told lies, gossiped about others bearing false witness. I also wanted things that didn't belong to me, and therefore coveted what others had.

You may have noticed I skipped murder. The Bible is clear on that one as well and sometimes we try to justify ourselves, but hate for a brother, genetically or a brother in Christ, is murder.

1 John 3:15
Whoever hates his brother is a murderer, and you know that no murderer has eternal life abiding in him.

Now I'd mentioned in my previous book I've never hated anyone. For some reason God has blessed me with the gift of not holding a grudge, so forgiveness comes very easy for me. But like all men I've been tempted to hate others, and still am tempted, and could easily fall into sin should I allow the world to influence me.

As you can see, I've had my share of sin, shame and guilt. I don't dwell on any of it. Again, I'm sharing to make anyone reading this aware that I'm not here to sit in judgement or make accusations. There's plenty that I've done that makes me grateful for a forgiving God.

A God that calls out to each of us, has granted me forgiveness, will grant you forgiveness, welcome you to His kingdom, if only you would repent, receive Him as your Lord and Savior, and then follow Him based on His word. A few simple steps towards an eternal salvation that can change your whole outlook on your life here, now, and forevermore.

Romans 10:9
that if you confess with your mouth the Lord Jesus and believe in your heart that God has raised Him from the dead, you will be saved.

Leviticus 19:1-3

And the Lord spoke to Moses, saying, "Speak to all the congregation of the children of Israel, and say to them: 'You shall be holy, for I the Lord your God am holy. 'Every one of you shall revere his mother and his father, and keep My Sabbaths: I *am* the Lord your God.

The Current Culture and Moral Decay

It has become increasingly obvious that there is something wrong with our culture. What we see coming through our media, via television, the internet, and most forms of communication seem to focus on the worst in our society. Many of the day and prime time shows, and movies, depict and glorify behavior that I would never have imagined in my lifetime.

It's gotten increasingly more difficult to watch TV without some show glorifying some type of sin whether it's lying, cheating, stealing, sexual sin, or murder. In many cases, the name of the show will tell you what sin they are focusing on, or glorifying.

Now I like to watch Sci-Fi shows and movies, and for the most part a good detective show is also of interest, as they are trying to figure out, whodunit. Yet, today's shows are graphic beyond need, as if the producers feel that the audience needs a fix of sexual innuendo or content, cursing, gore and mayhem to add shock value.

I am sure we have given them the impression, and justification, to produce these shows by turning them into ratings stars instead of shunning them when they appear. As we all know much of what is developed for TV, and the movies, are based on the desire for money and profit. If it isn't watched, or it doesn't sell, then it doesn't get produced.

What are we to do when all the sin we can easily, and readily, imagine in our own minds show up on our home TV screen? For a Christian we should know, and understand, that watching these sins played out on our screens would not please the Lord. Yet, it seems we can't, or won't, turn elsewhere for entertainment or diversion.

Should we, the Christian community, turn off the TV, computer, tablet, phones, etc.? I'll admit I've not been able to do that in many situations in my own life, so I can't honestly say to anyone to do that without being hypocritical. I'm getting better, but nowhere near where I need to be.

1 John 1:8
If we say that we have no sin, we deceive ourselves, and the truth is not in us.

I have gotten more selective in my viewing habits. Anything over PG-13, or TV-14, for the most part is a no go, but even then, there are also challenges with those ratings.   I'm fairly faithful to that because when I've not been diligent and watched an R rated, or TV-MA movie, it's been horrendous. In many cases I feel guilt, or experience sleepless nights, due to being disturbed in my spirit over the content that I've watched.

Psalm 119:37
Turn away my eyes from looking at worthless things, *And* revive me in Your way.

Although I'm coming from a Christian perspective, I have to wonder about those that profess to follow other religions that also condemn these sins? How could anyone, of any religion, watch these things, and not be offended, or realize they are failing and not following the dictates of their faith? All religions have moral directives and define sin. I can't honestly let anyone of any faith, or religion, off the hook on this particular issue.

Let's also address the so-called atheist or agnostic. Not believing, or not knowing whether to believe in God isn't a license for moral decay. If as an atheist, someone professes to be more enlightened than to believe in God, where does this leave them? Without a moral compass to guide them, are they so enlightened, or superior, that they don't see the decay of morality as an issue?

An atheist obviously doesn't believe that there are consequences for bad or evil behavior, from God. They do know if they break man's laws there could be consequences from government or law enforcement, but I wonder if they assume lying, cheating, adultery, and other similar sins are okay as long as they aren't caught?

In my worldview, the Christian worldview, I'm guilty of breaking God's laws even if I don't get caught. I believe in a real heaven and a real hell, and in the atheist's worldview, there is no heaven or hell. One of us is wrong, but in my worldview, there are no consequences if I'm wrong, but if they are wrong it will make an eternal difference.

The few people that I've known, or have heard profess, to be atheists have some moral values, so the question in my mind is where do they get their morality? Morality isn't just handed down, or inherited, it comes from somewhere.

Some might say it came from their parents, but then the question still lingers where did they get it? Some might say that it comes from inside of us, but how is that possible? If it's internal to us, it can only be possible if it was placed inside of us because unlike other things that are observable, morality while internal can be ignored.

Scripture tells us the law of God is written in our hearts. Our conscience bears witness to the law of God working in us, and accuses, or excuses, our behavior against the laws placed in us by God.

Romans 2:15
who show the work of the law written in their hearts, their conscience also bearing witness, and between themselves *their* thoughts accusing or else excusing *them*

So, the question of where morality comes from is best answered by scripture, and has been placed in us by a moral, righteous God. That is why our conscience also works, and strives, to be without offense. Although we can deny, and say we don't believe in God, what He has placed in us, our conscience, also works towards men. We try to live moral lives within society among others because of God's law written in our hearts. We can also ignore those laws and live according to our own desires.

Acts 24:16
This *being* so, I myself always strive to have
a conscience without offense toward God and men.

Let's then look at the agnostic. They on the other
hand, not being sure whether to believe there is a
God, are in a similar predicament, in my mind, as
an atheist. Since the agnostic is not sure there is a
God, but knows that he could potentially be wrong,
is in an extremely fragile state.

Then I have to wonder, how do they deal with life's
difficulties and challenges? When hurting,
doubting, ill, or in trouble, do they wonder if they
should pray, or seek God? If they take some action,
and pray, but God doesn't appear to answer, do they
just say, that's what I expected, and move on?

The agnostic, by not making up their mind, is in the
same situation as the atheist, and their eternal soul is
also at stake. Being unable, or unwilling, to commit
doesn't clear you from God's judgement.

In scripture, in the book of Revelation, God calls on
the church of the Laodiceans to either be cold, or
hot, or he would vomit them out of His mouth.
There must be a decision, or a choice, because there
are eternal consequences, or benefits.

Revelation 3:16
So then, because you are lukewarm, and neither
cold nor hot, I will vomit you out of My mouth

The rest of us that don't identify as atheists, or
agnostics, then have some kind of faith, belief,

religion, or whatever we want to call it now. Many atheists and agnostics claim a belief in science, or evolution, and what is often referred to as the "big bang." But when scrutinized this a belief in something, although they may not want to call it faith, it does take faith to believe that somehow mankind was able to figure out, through unproven scientific "theories," how the world came to be.

So, what is a theory in its simplest definition?

A theory is a group of linked ideas intended to explain something. A theory provides a framework for explaining observations. The explanations are based on assumptions. From the assumptions follows a number of possible hypotheses which can be tested to provide support for, or challenge, the theory. If it can't be tested to a satisfactory conclusion then it's merely an unproven theory.

I'm thinking a person really has to have a lot of faith to stake their eternal soul on the ability of flawed man to explain creation. They are accepting a bunch of ideas and assumptions made by man, to explain what supposedly could have happened billions of years ago, and observations that can't be duplicated or proven. If you have been around long enough you have heard what happens when you assume. This is definitely not a pretty picture, and my heart goes out to those caught up in this confusion.

I'll take my chances with God's word, the Bible, that has been around far longer than any of us in this day and age, and has been proven historically accurate over and over again. God's word is His revelation of his nature and character to us. God is who He claims to be.

Exodus 3:14
And God said to Moses, "I AM WHO I AM." And He said, "Thus you shall say to the children of Israel, 'I AM has sent me to you.'"

I've heard some very good Christian leaders speak about there being only two religions. The first time I heard this was from Ken Ham from the Answers In Genesis ministry.

He points out that one religion is based on man's worldview. This worldview, created by men, includes evolution, atheism, agnosticism, as well as all other religions outside of Christianity. The other religion is based on God's word, the Christian worldview. The conclusion is that it all boils down to only two options, man's worldview or God's worldview.

So, if you believe in the Bible, and that it is the inerrant word of God, then the above is an accurate statement, since it all boils down eventually to someone being right, and someone being wrong.

There are never going to be more than these two options to the question of faith and what a person believes in. If you believe every religion leads to God then you are wrong. The true God of the universe would find a way to reveal himself to us, and has done so through His word, the Bible.

Would a wise, powerful, and omnipotent God, not have a plan to reveal who He is? Wouldn't He have a plan that makes sense of the world? The confusion we are experiencing in our world today is because we refuse to believe His revelation to us through His word. In our refusal of His word we have opened ourselves up to demonic forces that rule over our world.

God's word is clear, we are sinners because of the sin of Adam in Genesis, the first book of the Bible, and we are in need salvation. There is only one way to receive that salvation and it is through Jesus Christ.

Yet, both the believer in Christ, and the non-believer, each believes they are right, but then how can that be? Satan has been corrupting God's plan from the beginning, and we have missed identifying his many delusions and schemes. He deceives us through false religions, makes men doubt that God is, and gives us alternatives that nurture, and drive our own desires. We are driven away from the truth because we have our own desires that we feel a need to satisfy, and those desires numb our senses, and our conscience.

Maybe I'm getting too deep into all of this, but take a look around, and tell me that we aren't seeing a decay in our morality, and in civility towards one another. We are fascinated with social media, streaming videos, TV news, and all the things that people do wrong. We have people out there that portray right and good behavior, but the ones that catch our attention most are the ones that show the worst in people, especially in our media, and what is being portrayed on our TV shows.

I do remember a day when a father figure on a television show was respected, and sought after for advice and guidance. I remember when mothers were portrayed as loving, and kind, and children were respectful, and obedient. Sure, it wasn't always reality, but the portrayals are now all extremes in the opposite direction.

Sexuality was modest and confined to good taste between a man and woman, male and female. Violence was shown in a way that didn't glorify evil, but today there's both extreme sexual content and violence shown, and exploited just for its own sake, whether relevant, or necessary to a plot.

Now I know some people will protest and say that we see plenty of good in people, but keep in mind the Bible tells us we are all sinners. So, for arguments sake let's ignore that, and agree, and say, yes, we see good in people, especially when disaster strikes. But like all things it's for a season, and doesn't last. Once life goes back to normal where we aren't facing tragedies, or difficulties, we go back to the numbing life of complacency.

In times of true needs, and disasters, many of the organizations that stay behind doing good works are faith-based, and committed to an effort even after the original tragedy has ended, and no longer in the media's radar. The media's interest dies after it's no longer newsworthy. Imagine for a moment that there are no faith-based ministries there to assist people in their time of need. What would the world look like? I'm thinking that with all its flaws, without the Christian church, the world would be a much gloomier place.

We use the term secular a lot to describe the decline in the influence of religion, or religious values. In loose terms we have seen a greater belief in human self-sufficiency, over the last few decades, as our society has become more affluent, and the belief that we, mankind, can solve all the ills of the world. The only problem is that there is one thing we can't solve, and that is our sin nature. Without a savior we are doomed to repeat our mistakes. We will always lie, steal, cheat, covet, and give in to all sexual desires imaginable to please our lusts.

That sounds like a very grim view of things, but there is a hope that defies understanding, and is available to each of us, but only if you seek Him. That hope is the salvation provided by our Lord and Savior, Jesus Christ, who died on a cross for our sins, rose from the grave, and is seated at the right hand of God the Father, to make a way for us to inherit a heavenly kingdom, when we finally leave this world upon our physical death.

1 John 5:2

By this we know that we love the children of God, when we love God and keep His commandments.

Delusion #1 – Identity

As I've prayed about what to write in this book, and what the Lord would have me share, He has given me several topics that have been revealed primarily in my dreams. The Lord has often worked in my life through dreams.

While living in Miami, Florida, and trying to find a way to provide for my family, I started to focus on teaching software applications such as Word, Excel, and other office products. I wasn't great with any of these, but when I was stumped on something that I couldn't figure out, and the instructions didn't make sense, I would get the answers in my dreams, and be able to teach others.

For several years I worked primarily as a contractor, and during that time I was very focused on the Lord, and His word. Throughout those years the Lord led my ways, and gave me knowledge that allowed me to learn software applications. That knowledge eventually opened an opportunity for employment in Information Technology as a career, and the source of God's provision for my family.

I know some people would be skeptical of someone professing they hear from God in their dreams, but that's how the Lord has worked in my life, so I'm comfortable, and confident, in His revelations to me, so I'll share what I've been given.

The first delusion that the Lord has shown me is that Satan, the devil himself, has been able to cause confusion is us as we have searched for identity, as well as meaning, and purpose, for our lives. Our need to feel significant, and unique, has been used to delude us in our search for purpose. What the devil has managed to do is to have us question who we are, not in light of who God says we are, but in light of our own desires for significance and purpose.

When we look at scripture, we often only see what we are taught, but how often do we seek God to get a full understanding of what the scriptures can reveal to us? I know from my own experience I take a lot for granted including the scripture that is most often quoted, or pronounced, from the gospel of John. It's read, or given to us, as if it's something we should automatically know, or understand, but God's word should never be taken lightly.

God's word is His love letter to us, and in taking a look at John 3:16-17, I can truly see the love that God has for us. A love that we can't truly comprehend, understand, or imagine.

John 3:16-17
16 For God so loved the world that He gave His only begotten Son, that whoever believes in Him should not perish but have everlasting life. 17 For God did not send His Son into the world to condemn the world, but that the world through Him might be saved.

Looking at the above scripture, we should understand that God loves us so much, He was willing to sacrifice His Son to give us everlasting life. I don't have any understanding, or concept of what that took, to send Jesus to His death, or of the everlasting life promised. But to know that Jesus was sent to do that for me, and you, and not to condemn us, which He has every right to do, is just so amazing. Given the sacrifice made by Jesus, our identity should be that we are children of God, as quoted in 1 John below.

1 John 3:1
Behold what manner of love the Father has bestowed on us, that we should be called children of God! Therefore the world does not know us, because it did not know Him.

In looking at scripture, I can't help but look at the first time the Lord established our identity.

Genesis 1:27
27 So God created mankind in his own image, in the image of God he created them; male and female he created them.

The verse above couldn't be any clearer. In creating us, the Lord was very precise, the first thing to note, and identify with, is that He made us in **His** own image. I don't understand how we can overlook such an important verse, and not realize that in creating us, God had a much greater plan for us because we were created to identify with Him. We have neglected our heritage and birthright!

The next thing that is clear is that there were no other sexual genders designed. So why are some Christians confused about this? To put it simply, it's because they have placed their own beliefs, or man's word, above the nature and character of God, and above the word of God.

When someone professing Christian faith, is not trusting and putting the word of God above man's word or knowledge, are we to assume that they are saved? Many might say I would be wrong to question a man's faith, or salvation, possibly say I'm being judgmental. But then again, how do we know to reach out, and point people in the right direction, correct wrong thinking, unless we question?

The apostle Paul in many of his writings to the various churches questioned them, so that they could think through what they believed, and ensure they were acting upon God's word.

Galatians 3:1-3
O foolish Galatians! Who has bewitched you that you should not obey the truth, before whose eyes Jesus Christ was clearly portrayed among you as crucified? ² This only I want to learn from you: Did you receive the Spirit by the works of the law, or by the hearing of faith? ³ Are you so foolish? Having begun in the Spirit, are you now being made perfect by the flesh?

In the book of 2 Timothy, Paul made it clear the we should put God's word above all others when he clearly stated that scripture is inspired by God, is profitable, and to be used for correction and instruction.

2 Timothy 3:16
All Scripture *is* given by inspiration of God,
and *is* profitable for doctrine, for reproof,
for correction, for instruction in righteousness,

Yes, we should give anyone professing Christ as their Savior, the benefit of the doubt, that they are saved. On the other hand, we must also be discerning, and use God's word to get people walking in a manner that agrees with their profession of faith.

There are some things we need to consider in light of God's word, and they are a man's actions, to determine if they align with God's word. God's word also tells us that those that are His bear good fruit. In other words, they share His word, and bring people to the saving knowledge, grace and mercy of Jesus Christ.

Matthew 7:18-20
[18] A good tree cannot bear bad fruit, nor *can* a bad tree bear good fruit. [19] Every tree that does not bear good fruit is cut down and thrown into the fire. [20] Therefore by their fruits you will know them.

But getting back to my focus on identity? Let's look at mankind's struggle with identity since the beginning. In Genesis, when Eve was tempted, why was she deceived? Simply put she was tempted by her own desires.

James 1:14
But each one is tempted when he is drawn away by his own desires and enticed.

Genesis 3:4
[4] Then the serpent said to the woman, "You will not surely die. [5] For God knows that in the day you eat of it your eyes will be opened, and **you will be like God**, knowing good and evil."

I've highlighted in bold the words above for emphasize, to show that the serpent deceived her by telling her she "**will be like God**." What is it about us that we want to be more than God made us to be? God made us in His image, not to be like Him. So, what's the difference? We are created beings, and as part of the creation we will always have limitations.

As an omnipotent, omnipresent, all powerful being, God is above, and beyond, our capabilities and understanding. Being made in His image we can reach the potential God intended for us, which is not to be like Him, but to righteousness, which is a right standing with Him, and that only comes through the salvation offered through Jesus Christ.

In the book of Psalm, the psalmist wondered, and asked the question, "What is man?"

Psalm 8:4

[4] What is man that You are mindful of him,
And the son of man that You visit him?

The above Psalm was repeated in the New
Testament in the book of Hebrews.

Hebrews: 2:6

"What is man that You are mindful of him,
Or the son of man that You take care of him?

The answer isn't always obvious. I've often called
out to the Lord and asked, why are you so good to
me Lord, why have you blessed me when I'm
always disappointing you? It always comes back to
what God says in His word at the beginning of John
3:16, "For God so loved the world."

Do I understand that love, or can I make sense of it,
and find a way to interpret it? No, it's beyond my
comprehension, but I accept it as truth and many,
many, many times have felt His love, and it makes
me cry in appreciation, and I'm thankful for having
a loving God.

I also realize that God the Father sent Jesus to
answer the question once and for all, "What is
man?" Looking at scripture in the end of Hebrews
2 we see that Jesus came as a man, to be our High
Priest, the propitiation, atoning sacrifice, for our
sins, and to aid us who are tempted.

Hebrews 2:17-18

[17] Therefore, in all things He had to be made like *His* brethren, that He might be a merciful and faithful High Priest in things *pertaining* to God, to make propitiation for the sins of the people. [18] For in that He Himself has suffered, being tempted, He is able to aid those who are tempted.

So, let me get back to the thoughts on the culture and what has happened over the last few decades. Again, reading Genesis 1:27, where God made man in His image, He also states "male and female he created them."

Our culture now says people are born that way, meaning gay, lesbian, etc., even Christians are believing this lie. This lie also goes against the identity that the Lord gave us, "male and female," and is an affront to God's word.

When the term homosexual is used in scripture it is used to describe sin, not a person, or a biological sex. The word is not used as a contrast for sexual preference, but as a sin.

1 Corinthians 6:9-10

[9] Do you not know that the unrighteous will not inherit the kingdom of God? Do not be deceived. Neither fornicators, nor idolaters, nor adulterers, nor homosexuals, nor [sodomites, [10] nor thieves, nor covetous, nor drunkards, nor revilers, nor extortioners will inherit the kingdom of God.

Let's keep in mind that the first known appearance of the word *homosexual* in print is found in an 1869 German pamphlet. In scripture, it was added to refer to sin in the newer Bible translations, but the King James Version reads as follows:

Corinthians 6:9-10 (KJV)

[9] Know ye not that the unrighteous shall not inherit the kingdom of God? Be not deceived: neither fornicators, nor idolaters, nor adulterers, nor effeminate, nor abusers of themselves with mankind, [10] Nor thieves, nor covetous, nor drunkards, nor revilers, nor extortioners, shall inherit the kingdom of God.

In today's culture the word homosexual is now used to describe an individual preferring a same sex partner. It refers to a lifestyle choice, and even many professing Christians have determined, it is no longer sin. But looking at the verse in the scriptures above it's not listed there as a lifestyle, or gender. It is simply sin, among a series of other sins.

How is it possible that anyone could interpret the word homosexual as a gender? Simply put it's because many have denied the authority of the Bible in their lives. I have to come back to the question I've asked before; how can they call themselves Christian, if they deny the authority of God's word? We have lost our understanding of who God is, and whom the word Christian is supposed to identify with, and that is the Lord Jesus Christ.

Rather than get into a whole history lesson let's just agree that the word, homosexual, hasn't been around as long as the Bible, or scripture overall. My point is that a word that was referring to sin in scripture, has been changed by man to refer to sexual preference or behavior. When it was placed in scripture it was intended to describe sin and nothing more.

When a Bible believing Christian uses the words homosexual, transsexual, bisexual and other similar words used to describe sexual preference, or sexuality, we are referring to sin, or sinful behavior, versus a person or group of people.

What has occurred in the LGBT community is that they have taken ownership of those titles, and labels, as part of their identity. In doing so they have effectively made any negative connotation an attack, or supposed hate crime, against their community. It is now called hate to speak against what a Christian refers to as a sinful act. They have been very clever in reframing words that previously described sin to make it appear as an attack on their identity.

Ultimately that's the key, identity. Our entire lives revolve around identity and we've made a mess by creating more ways to identify ourselves.

When we look at scripture, we see references throughout that refer to the names of the ancestors and tribes of various people groups. While the scriptures do use terms to identify these groups, and people, they are primarily used to give historical and generational context as well as to identify, and separate, those that followed, or did not follow God.

In society we use multiple terms to identify ourselves, some of which have nothing to do with our true identity. I'm a father, grandfather, uncle, cousin, and other terms describing my standing in my family by birth.

I also use terms such as Manager, Church Member, Association member, etc., to describe roles I have, or play, in the world. But those roles don't define my identity, (although some people may identify with what they do in the world, or their jobs, as their identity), they clarify a position I hold to identify my place in something that may be temporary, or a role given to me, but not necessarily dealing with my birthright.

Identifying our birthright is a very different matter. When we identify ourselves, our birthright in Jesus Christ should be our focus, not the terms used by man. What I'm getting at is that our birthright as a Christian comes as a result of our profession of faith in Christ, and our being "reborn" in Christ. We are then heirs, and sons, but only through our rebirth in Christ.

Paul understood the seriousness of who we are in Christ when he corrected the Corinthian church. He understood the consequences when people separate themselves by identifying with man, instead of identifying with Christ as our Lord and Savior.

1 Corinthians 3:4-8
[4] For when one says, "I am of Paul," and another, "I *am* of Apollos," are you not carnal?
[5] Who then is Paul, and who *is* Apollos, but ministers through whom you believed, as the Lord gave to each one? [6] I planted, Apollos watered, but God gave the increase. [7] So then neither he who plants is anything, nor he who waters, but God who gives the increase. [8] Now he who plants and he who waters are one, and each one will receive his own reward according to his own labor.

In our physical world we forget that no matter what we label, or call ourselves, the one thing we can't change is our birthright. I look in the mirror and see a man, and even if I want to deny it my body parts are those of a man. My mind can be confused, and I can try to change my looks by dressing differently, get surgery to alter my body parts, but that doesn't change anything except what I see in the mirror. The enemy tempts us, then lies to us about who we are, and once we start to believe the lie, we fall into sin.

When Paul saw that the church was being divided by identifying with a certain person, or idea, he quickly addressed it. Paul states that there is no Paul or Apollos, "So then neither he who plants is anything, nor he who waters," they are nothing, there's only God, who gives the increase leading people to Christ."

We are all born into some birthright, or heritage, when we first come into this world, like it or not. When we repent and give our lives to Jesus Christ, we have a new birthright, a new identity. We are "born again" and then sealed with Christ, and we are no longer slaves to sin, or slaves to our lusts, desires, and political correctness.

What does any of this have to do with the LGBT, or homosexual community, or those that refer to themselves as "Gay Christians?" Why everything of course! There is only one identity in Christ. You can't be a gay Christian, any more than you can be a black, white, Indian, Chinese, or any other noun or pronoun you want to use in front of Christ, it's not possible!

Here's a question, and concern, in my mind. Why has the Christian church, for centuries fallen into the same pattern of identifying themselves in other terms? How many times have you heard Christians refer to themselves in terms of their denomination? The Lord didn't create denominations, man did, and he also didn't create the term non denomination to describe those that didn't want to fit into those molds.

We either belong to Christ, or we do not. Any term that adds to a person being a follower of Jesus Christ ties that person's identity first to the term they use, but not to Christ. Christ was clear when He said.

Luke 16:13
[13] "No servant can serve two masters; for either he will hate the one and love the other, or else he will be loyal to the one and despise the other. You cannot serve God and mammon."

Although he finishes here with mammon, material wealth or possessions, this principle applies to our serving God in our lives. In the previous verses, in Luke 16 (see below), the Lord Jesus also makes this principle clear in our loyalties and faithfulness. If we as Christian's cannot be faithful in what God has entrusted us, His word, to be faithful to it, and believe, and share it, as He has defined it, how will he trust us in His true riches?

Luke 16:10-12
[10] He who *is* faithful in *what is* least is faithful also in much; and he who is unjust in *what is* least is unjust also in much. [11] Therefore if you have not been faithful in the unrighteous mammon, who will commit to your trust the true *riches?* [12] And if you have not been faithful in what is another man's, who will give you what is your own?

In the latter part of Acts 11:26 we find the first use of the word Christian, in reference to the disciples of Jesus Christ. The next time it is used is in Acts 26:28 after Paul had just given his testimony to King Agrippa and others.

Acts 11:26
And when he had found him, he brought him to Antioch. So it was that for a whole year they assembled with the church and taught a great many people. And the disciples were first called Christians in Antioch.

Acts 26:28
Then Agrippa said to Paul, "You almost persuade me to become a Christian."

Here we have a clear understanding that the term Christian was used for followers of Jesus Christ. But then the question is raised, who is a follower of Jesus Christ?

In most churches today we hear an altar call to repent, and profess Jesus as Lord and Savior, and be saved. Many people have done that throughout the ages, yet none of us can truly know what's in a person's heart, and soul, when they do that. We know that Judas Iscariot walked as a disciple of Jesus, yet betrayed Him.

Mark 14:10
Then Judas Iscariot, one of the twelve, went to the chief priests to betray Him to them.

So, what is that distinction, I'm trying to make here? Where did Jesus draw, or define, the line for those that are truly following Him?

Jesus was very clear, when He told his disciples to follow Him, what was expected of them. Those that don't take up his cross are not worthy of Him. They must deny themselves, and store up treasures in heaven. They shall not walk in darkness and they hear His voice.

Matthew 10:38
And he who does not take his cross and follow after Me is not worthy of Me.

Matthew 16:24
Then Jesus said to His disciples, "If anyone desires to come after Me, let him deny himself, and take up his cross, and follow Me.

Matthew 19:21
Jesus said to him, "If you want to be perfect, go, sell what you have and give to the poor, and you will have treasure in heaven; and come, follow Me."

John 8:12
Then Jesus spoke to them again, saying, "I am the light of the world. He who follows Me shall not walk in darkness, but have the light of life."

John 10:27
My sheep hear My voice, and I know them, and they follow Me.

How many of us can truly say the Lord speaks to me, and I hear, and follow His voice? Do I deny my rights, lay down my life, and put others before me, and give to those in need? Do I pick up my cross, and follow Jesus wherever He leads? When can we say, I will not stumble because I walk in His light, and though I die, there is no other course for me to take, but the course laid out for me by Jesus, my Lord and Savior?

I know from my own experience that I'm still not there, and yet I know in me that it is my desire to do His will, and follow Him. As Paul so clearly put it.

Romans 7:18-25
[18] For I know that in me (that is, in my flesh) nothing good dwells; for to will is present with me, but *how* to perform what is good I do not find. [19] For the good that I will *to do,* I do not do; but the evil I will not *to do,* that I practice. [20] Now if I do what I will not *to do,* it is no longer I who do it, but sin that dwells in me.
[21] I find then a law, that evil is present with me, the one who wills to do good. [22] For I delight in the law of God according to the inward man. [23] But I see another law in my members, warring against the law of my mind, and bringing me into captivity to the law of sin which is in my members. [24] O wretched man that I am! Who will deliver me from this body of death? [25] I thank God—through Jesus Christ our Lord!

Paul was so clear, the things I want to do, turn away from watching, speaking, or thinking, things that don't glorify or honor God, those things I don't always do. The battle is always raging and my good intentions are often not good enough. Thank God, that Jesus is in my life to deliver me!

When I go through trials, and areas of questioning where I am with the Lord, I'm often reminded of the parable of the sower. I've always wanted to be that sower who bears good fruit, but I often feel like I've not been planted on good and fertile ground.

Matthew 13:18-23

[18] "Therefore hear the parable of the sower: [19] When anyone hears the word of the kingdom, and does not understand *it,* then the wicked *one* comes and snatches away what was sown in his heart. This is he who received seed by the wayside. [20] But he who received the seed on stony places, this is he who hears the word and immediately receives it with joy; [21] yet he has no root in himself, but endures only for a while. For when tribulation or persecution arises because of the word, immediately he stumbles. [22] Now he who received seed among the thorns is he who hears the word, and the cares of this world and the deceitfulness of riches choke the word, and he becomes unfruitful. [23] But he who received seed on the good ground is he who hears the word and understands *it,* who indeed bears fruit and produces: some a hundredfold, some sixty, some thirty."

In the verses above we see Jesus explaining the different types of people that the sower, anyone who shares God's word with another, comes into contact with. The first type of person doesn't understand what he hears, and the devil snatches it away. The second person receives it with joy, knows it's true, but didn't commit himself to knowing God, and His word, and when tribulations and persecution comes won't be able to stand. The third hears it, gets it, but is busy with success, and other endeavors, so that the word, the Bible, sits on

His lampstand as a decoration, and never shares God's love. The fourth hears, understands and shares God's word, produces Christian's that love the Lord.

The last one that is referred to is the one that identifies with God. His identity is founded on the knowledge of God's word. He knows that God created the heavens, the earth, and man and woman. He doesn't doubt, doesn't waver, and is assured of the rewards laid up for him in God's kingdom. My prayer is that you won't be deceived by the ways, and words of the world, and that you'll find your identity in God, the creator of all things, including you.

Scriptures to consider when seeking to
identify who you are in Christ:

Psalm 14:2
The Lord looks down from heaven upon the
children of men,
To see if there are any who understand, who seek
God.

Matthew 6:26
Look at the birds of the air, for they neither sow nor
reap nor gather into barns; yet your heavenly Father
feeds them. Are you not of more value than they?

Luke 12:7
But the very hairs of your head are all numbered.
Do not fear therefore; you are of more value than
many sparrows.

Luke 12:24
Consider the ravens, for they neither sow nor reap,
which have neither storehouse nor barn; and God
feeds them. Of how much more value are you than
the birds?

Luke 4:43
but He said to them, "I must preach the kingdom of
God to the other cities also, because for this purpose
I have been sent."

John 1:12
But as many as received Him, to them He gave the
right to become children of God, to those who
believe in His name:

Romans 8:16
The Spirit Himself bears witness with our spirit that we are children of God,

Romans 8:17
and if children, then heirs—heirs of God and joint heirs with Christ, if indeed we suffer with *Him,* that we may also be glorified together

1 John 2:28
And now, little children, abide in Him, that when He appears, we may have confidence and not be ashamed before Him at His coming.

1 John 3:2
Beloved, now we are children of God; and it has not yet been revealed what we shall be, but we know that when He is revealed, we shall be like Him, for we shall see Him as He is.

Deuteronomy 11:1

Therefore you shall love the Lord your God, and keep His charge, His statutes, His judgments, and His commandments always.

Delusion #2 – It's About Love

Another very well-crafted delusion is around the concept that the homosexual, gay, lesbian, etc., lifestyle is about love. The question often posed is that since God is love how could this be wrong? They argue that God, created all of us, and He knew they were born that way.

Psalm 139:13
For You formed my inward parts; You covered me in my mother's womb.

The scripture above makes it clear God formed us, and God does know us from our mother's womb. But scripture also is clear that God made us male and female, and there is no other gender, as I discussed in the previous chapter.

The problem is that people don't want to accept God's word and refuse to listen to truth. In deciding on how to address this issue of love, I had been reflecting on my approach during my drive to work, while listening to American Family Radio, a Christian radio station.

I usually enjoy listening to Sandy Rios in the Morning. In the introduction of her radio talk show, she makes two statements that I thought may be appropriate, since I'm going to offend people with my next couple of statements. The first statement made on her show's introduction each morning is, "we're not called to be nice" and the other is "we are often called to be confrontational."

So, here are my not nice and confrontational statements. Same sex relationships, dressing up like a woman, and having sex with partners of both sexes is sin, pure and simple. As a Christian there is no way to accept, or defend, this lifestyle, and I'm not going to sugar coat it by calling this love.

I know the above appears to be combative, but there isn't any good way to express the truth without offense. That being said I'd like to share some practical thoughts.

I believe a man can love a man, and a woman love another woman. But the Lord placed very specific parameters around that kind of love, and it excludes the sexual aspects.

Leviticus 18:22
You shall not lie with a male as with a woman. It *is* an abomination.

Romans 1:26-27
[26] For this reason God gave them up to vile passions. For even their women exchanged the natural use for what is against nature. [27] Likewise also the men, leaving the natural use of the woman, burned in their lust for one another, men with men committing what is shameful, and receiving in themselves the penalty of their error which was due.

In my first book I wrote about my love for my best friend, but it is a pure love, based on a friendship that has endured throughout our lives. I do believe that when our thoughts cross that line, between love and lust, it's driven by other factors that have shaped our lives. There's a trigger, a temptation, that drives people to a particular sexual sin, and in its simplest form, it's called lust.

I also believe there is also a trigger that can help anyone find their way back from the sin of lust that they have chosen. I truly believe that seeking the Lord can be that trigger, giving the sinner a new desire, for deliverance, from their sexual sin.

When I think about God forming us, I also realize that He knows what we will aspire to do, which sin will attract, or draw us. In this particular case, it is around our sexual lusts and desires. What we must come to realize, and admit, is that it is still that person's choice, to choose, or deny the sin.

Scripture also tells us that we are all born sinners.

Romans 3:23
for all have sinned and fall short of the glory of God

Professing, or accepting, that there are other sexes, other than male or female, essentially denies the sovereignty of God. Not believing God's word, as the final authority, for the Christian is sin. Since we all are sinners, God made a way for us to overcome by providing us with a Savior. But in order to receive that salvation we must repent, and must turn to the only source of salvation, Jesus Christ. Only He can provide atonement for us, for the forgiveness of our sins. Yet turning to Jesus requires repentance, and repentance requires a change, but not acceptance of sin.

Acts 17:30
Truly, these times of ignorance God overlooked, but now commands all men everywhere to repent.

So, here's the issue, God knows us, we are all sinners, and we ALL need to repent. Saying someone is born this way, is no excuse. I was born a sinner, lied, cheated, committed adultery, and much more, but God isn't going to let me use, that I was born that way, as an excuse to continue to be those things, to continue in sin.

God's word is very clear and tells us that we are led astray by our own desires. That's the real issue that we place our own desires, feelings for others, and man's word, above God's word.

James 1:14
But each one is tempted when he is drawn away by his own desires and enticed.

Ultimately, God does not make us sinners, but we are born with a sin nature, that eventually leads us to choose the sin, or sins, we want, or will engage in.

The media has been telling us for decades now that this lifestyle is not sin, but that people are born this way. Of course, none of it is backed up by science, while there is ample proof, and studies, that reveal quite the opposite is true. Yet, I've come to realize that the proof, the truth, doesn't matter to people who want to do their own thing and follow their own will.

1 John 1:8

If we say that we have no sin, we deceive ourselves, and the truth is not in us.

If you profess to be a Christian, and if you believe the lie, that this lifestyle is not sin, then I will flat out tell you that you need to decide who you will serve, and who you will call father, God or the devil? If you have accepted what the world has told you instead of God's word then I must seriously ask, are you saved?

I know some Christian pastors and leaders may not agree with me, or will not challenge someone with that question, but if we don't, then how do we bring people to repentance and salvation? You can only have one master, and he is either God, or the father of lies, Satan.

Jesus told the Jews questioning His authority, and identity, that they did not know God, but were children of the devil.

John 8:44

You are of *your* father the devil, and the desires of your father you want to do. He was a murderer from the beginning, and does not stand in the truth, because there is no truth in him. When he speaks a lie, he speaks from his own *resources,* for he is a liar and the father of it.

If you have chosen to believe the lie you need to repent, and get right with God.

So, who am I, that I can make such a bold statement? As stated before, I'm not a pastor, evangelist, teacher, prophet or anyone with worldly credentials. I'm just a father, praying for his child, and wanting to reach others with God's truth.

I do believe I've been called to give this message. Believe me I've fought writing this book, but the Lord has not given me release. I'm writing this out of love, not for anyone, or anything other than my Lord and Savior, Jesus Christ.

In the previous chapter I went over the fact that you can't serve two masters. Now let's talk about, true love, the love we need to have for God. Jesus made it clear.

Mark 12:29-31
29 Jesus answered him, "The first of all the commandments is: 'Hear, O Israel, the LORD our God, the LORD is one. 30 And you shall love the LORD your God with all your heart, with all your soul, with all your mind, and with all your strength.' This is the first commandment. 31 And the second, like it, is this: 'You shall love your neighbor as yourself.' There is no other commandment greater than these."

The first commandment is to love the Lord. To love God appears to be an obvious, and easy, statement to understand, but is it? What does it mean to most of us? I thought I understood it until I was faced with decisions in my life that showed me how little I truly understood what loving God meant. God must come first above anyone, or anything else, and it should be with everything in our heart, soul, mind and strength.

God has dealt with me on a couple of occasions regarding my love for my family, and my love for Him, Jesus Christ. The first time was dealing with my son. He had become very involved in the world, and I didn't know how to help him. I finally turned to the Lord, and asked Him to do with him whatever was necessary, to either straighten him out, or take him, before his life took a direction that would lead him astray. Today, my son is serving the Lord in ministry.

The second time, and still ongoing, has been dealing with my daughter, and her new lifestyle. I love my daughter, and thought I had completely turned her over to the Lord. What I've recently realized is that I was still holding onto something. She's my little girl, and each time I had prayed for her, it had been for God's protection.

For the past few years, I've been praying for the Lord to open her eyes to her sin, but also to keep her safe, and to protect her. I've come to realize that part of my prayers had been primarily to protect me, and her mother, from any hurt that could come because of this lifestyle. While seeming right, and holy, this type of prayer isn't what is necessary for her to come back to Christ in repentance.

This may seem harsh and unloving, but the reality is that as much as I love her, she doesn't need me to pray that way for her. She needs the Lord's discipline and correction. So, that has been the change in my prayers. Lord, do what you must do, whatever it takes. The Lord knows what she needs and I shouldn't, in any way, believe or pray otherwise.

Hebrews 12:11
Now no chastening seems to be joyful for the present, but painful; nevertheless, afterward it yields the peaceable fruit of righteousness to those who have been trained by it.

2 Timothy 3:16
All Scripture *is* given by inspiration of God, and *is* profitable for doctrine, for reproof, for correction, for instruction in righteousness,

I'm sure, if you are a parent praying for a wayward child, you are thinking this is a hard thing to do. Loving our children enough to ask for God's discipline, and correction, is the only way to truly show your trust and love, for the Lord, who wants the best for all of us. There have been times when I've questioned myself, but it all becomes clear when we follow Jesus' command on how to love God. Our love must be with our whole heart, mind, soul, and strength.

The last part of this command, strength, is the one in the list that doesn't seem to get much focus, or discussion, but it does take strength to love God the way he requires of us. I've also come to the realization that strength also comes from the Lord, to not only deal with the challenges of life, but also in the moments of crises in our lives.

Psalm 18:2

The Lord is my rock and my fortress and my deliverer; My God, my strength, in whom I will trust; My shield and the horn of my salvation, my stronghold.

It's interesting that the Lord is also referred to as "my strength," which means for those who trust in Him, He will be our shield, salvation, and stronghold.

Psalm 31:24

Be of good courage, And He shall strengthen your heart, All you who hope in the Lord.

In addition, the Lord strengthens our heart. The Lord will get us through each of these moments in our lives, where there is sadness, pain, grief, or loss, if only we make up our minds to know who He truly is, His nature and character, and ultimately determine who He is in our lives.

When Jesus was facing His final moments, after He was betrayed, but before He was taken into custody, we read the following:

Luke 22:42-44

42 saying, "Father, if it is Your will, take this cup away from Me; nevertheless, not My will, but Yours, be done." 43Then an angel appeared to Him from heaven, strengthening Him. 44 And being in agony, He prayed more earnestly. Then His sweat became like great drops of blood falling down to the ground.

In the scripture above when Jesus prayed to His Father to, "take this cup away from Me," He knew what was ahead. A brutal, painful, and horrific death. His Father didn't answer that prayer by removing the judgement that was required for our sin. The Father sent an angel to strengthen Him, so that He could do what was required for our salvation. What an awesome God we serve that in our moments of great needs, and difficulties in life, He can, and will be our strength.

Let's go back now and deal with the second part of the scripture we read earlier in this chapter which dealt with loving others.

Mark 12:31
³¹ And the second, like *it, is* this: **'You shall love your neighbor as yourself.'** There is no other commandment greater than these."

This scripture as well as Luke 10:27, which reads similar, are often also used to accuse or shame Christian's into accepting this lifestyle because we are then called unloving, towards our neighbors, or others.

Armed with those statements they have the nerve to question our Christianity, and we let them because we don't know how to defend our faith, and what scripture says.

So, let's look at the scriptures where Jesus spoke about who is our neighbor in answer to a question posed by a lawyer, someone that was an expert in the law.

Luke 10:29-37

29 But he, wanting to justify himself, said to Jesus, "And who is my neighbor?"

30 Then Jesus answered and said: "A certain *man* went down from Jerusalem to Jericho, and fell among thieves, who stripped him of his clothing, wounded *him,* and departed, leaving *him* half dead. **31** Now by chance a certain priest came down that road. And when he saw him, he passed by on the other side. **32** Likewise a Levite, when he arrived at the place, came and looked, and passed by on the other side. **33** But a certain Samaritan, as he journeyed, came where he was. And when he saw him, he had compassion. **34** So he went to *him* and bandaged his wounds, pouring on oil and wine; and he set him on his own animal, brought him to an inn, and took care of him. **35** On the next day, [i]when he departed, he took out two denarii, gave *them* to the innkeeper, and said to him, 'Take care of him; and whatever more you spend, when I come again, I will repay you.' **36** So which of these three do you think was neighbor to him who fell among the thieves?" **37** And he said, "He who showed mercy on him." Then Jesus said to him, "Go and do likewise."

When Jesus gave this answer about who is our "neighbor" you'll need to note that this man was not in sin, that we know of. He fell prey to others, thieves, and was wounded, needing help. This man was a neighbor in need of mercy.

The Lord does call us to have mercy on others which is shown by having compassion, towards someone when it is within our power to punish, harm or help. This man was shown compassion by his neighbor, the person who helped him, the Samaritan. What greater compassion can we have than to tell them of the salvation available in Jesus Christ.

So, when scripture tells us to love your neighbor it is telling us to have compassion on them. Let's show our compassion by telling them of the saving grace, and mercy, of Jesus Christ and His salvation. Our Lord in His mercy puts away our sin, when we turn to Him for salvation in repentance. Mercy and compassion does not mean that we are to excuse sin.

But let's say this man in the scripture above was in sin, and you caught him in that sin, what did Jesus say in scripture was His reason for coming? To call sinners to repentance. He never excused sin, but preached to them a message of repentance, offering them salvation. That is what we are called to do, to call sinners to repentance by sharing the gospel.

Matthew 4:17
From that time Jesus began to preach and to say, "Repent, for the kingdom of heaven is at hand."

Matthew 9:13
But go and learn what *this* means: 'I desire mercy and not sacrifice.' For I did not come to call the righteous, but sinners, to repentance."

So, who are the sinners, and the righteous, Jesus refers to in the verse above? Earlier in this chapter I noted that we are all sinners, and that all have sinned. Yet, here we have Jesus saying He was not calling the righteous, but sinners, to repentance. How is it possible, that scripture says we are all sinners, yet Jesus states that He is not calling the righteous to repentance? Are there righteous people that are not sinners?

The righteous that Jesus refers to here are those that in their own hearts, and mind, believe themselves to be above God's law and His word. It refers to the person that doesn't believe they are in sin, and therefore cannot, or will not, admit they are sinners. In their own minds they believe they are in a right standing with God.

You must understand, that unless you can identify yourself as a sinner, then you can't hear the call of Jesus Christ. If we say we have no sin, then we are basically saying, we don't need Christ, and therefore unable, or unwilling, to repent and accept His salvation.

Christian's calling sinners to repentance has now been described as judgmental, and I'll speak to that in the next chapter, but it's not judgement, but love. The love that Jesus calls us to have for our neighbor is to give them the gospel of salvation. If a person dies in their sin, they are doomed to an eternal separation from God. What is more loving, to share Christ, and tell someone they are sinners, with the hope of repentance, or let them die in their sin with no hope?

If you are a Christian that is allowing sin from those around you, if you truly love them, share Jesus, and call them to repentance. You can't make that decision for them, but there is a lot of regret when someone passes away, and you don't know whether they were saved, and wonder about their final outcome once they are gone.

So, let me share another story in my life. My earthly father abandoned my mother, and in kind the rest of us, four grown adults, two men and two women, and several grandchildren nearly 40 years ago.

I wasn't saved when he left, and in some ways, felt compassion for him since my mother at times could be challenging. I was going through my own struggles in my first marriage, so I was probably more sympathetic than upset.

My relationship with my father was never close, but I still loved him as my dad. We kept in touch, and I visited him in California a few times. We would talk about Jesus in general, but I never asked him what he understood, or knew about Jesus. I never asked him the question that was asked of me, by someone who loved God, and me, enough to find out where I stood in my understanding, and relationship, with Jesus Christ.

In 2015, my father called, and told me he had moved to New Mexico, and gave me his new address and phone number, but I never had the opportunity to visit him there. I would call him, and he would call me, maybe 2-3 times a year. We would speak briefly, usually I'd ask how he's doing, and he would say he's still alive and we would both laugh. To be honest, my main reason for calling was to see if he was still alive.

I spoke to him in the early part of 2016, but by the end of 2016, he no longer answered the phone number that he had given me. In some ways I reasoned, he may have moved again, and would possibly call me at some point. I tried the number several times over the next two years, and when there still was no answer, I assumed he had passed away.

Towards the end of 2018, my nephew did some research, and found out my father had passed away. Although, I suspected as much, it left me a little numb to know it was final. The first thing that struck me was that I did not know where he stood with Jesus, and I that had never shared the gospel with him.

Sure, I prayed with him when I visited. I also prayed throughout the years that someone would reach out to him, and share the gospel, but why didn't I? This is one of my biggest regrets, not knowing. I've buried my feelings on this deep inside, and all I can do right now is cry, and ask the Lord to forgive me, for not loving my earthly father enough to share the gospel with him.

In contrast there is comfort in knowing where someone stands with Christ when they pass away, which is where my friend Steve comes in. Steve was a coworker, but also a friend. We worked together nearly 16 years and shared adjacent offices for at least 10 of those years. Most mornings he would be the first face I'd see, and we got into the habit of greeting each other with, "how you doing?" and imagine that greeting in a Brooklyn accent.

Steve and I shared many moments in our lives throughout the years. We often spoke of, and shared, our faith. He often said to me, God comes, first, others next, and he was third. During the hurts of his divorce, we often cried, and prayed together. He was the first person, I shared, and cried with, about my daughter's decision to lead a same sex lifestyle.

In Oct 2018, my friend had a massive heart attack while at work. I saw him lying on the floor, and although I knelt, and prayed for him, I knew in my heart that he was already gone. In the emergency room, his wife, of only a few months, had to make the decision to stop treatment. She turned to me and asked what she should do, and while we cried together, I told her he was gone, and wouldn't want to stay plugged to machines.

I went over to his lifeless body, and as I stroked his face, and said goodbye, the Lord brought to mind a partial verse of scripture, "I shall go to him, but he shall not return to me." The Lord comforted me with this scripture from 2 Samuel 12, when King David's son died, with the knowledge that my friend was with Him, and that someday I would see him again. My friend is gone, and I still think of him, and miss him, but know where he is, and am assured that someday we'll celebrate together in heaven.

If you have anyone in your life that you have not shared the gospel with, and don't know where they stand, please, I beg you, settle this in your heart, and know. Love them enough to share Christ with them. Even if they decline, you'll at least have some closure knowing you tried, and the offer was made, and they made their choice known.

Yes, they may reject the gospel, but you plant the seed, and pray for someone to come along and water. God may work in their life, and may give the increase, if we do our part to share.

1 Corinthians 3:6-7
[6]I planted, Apollos watered, but God gave the increase. [7]So then neither he who plants is anything, nor he who waters, but God who gives the increase.

We need to be about our Father's business just like Jesus, loving God, loving people, sharing the gospel, and making disciples. This is a message, I've taken from the church we attend, and is clearly delivered, portrayed, and lived out throughout our church. It's been a constant reminder that sharing Jesus is how we show our love for God, for people, and that the sharing of the gospel is to call people to repentance.

Luke 24:46-47

84

⁴⁶ Then He said to them, "Thus it is written, and thus it was necessary for the Christ to suffer and to rise from the dead the third day, ⁴⁷ and that repentance and remission of sins should be preached in His name to all nations, beginning at Jerusalem.

Let's keep in mind that without repentance there is no remission, cancellation of the debt incurred, or forgiveness, for our sins. If we give the gospel without expecting repentance, where is the forgiveness, or payment of the debt? Jesus paid the debt, but repentance is required to receive that payment. Once someone truly repents the debt is settled.

I've often made excuses for not sharing the gospel. I would say to myself; they probably have already heard it. I would mention, or talk about Jesus, and used similar tactics, but not share the salvation message offered by Christ. My lack of faith, in believing the Lord for what He has told us explicitly to do, may have been that persons last chance for salvation. I need to be sure to share Jesus with the people the Lord puts in my path, since it may make an eternal difference in someone's life.

At the end of the book of Matthew, Jesus gave His instructions to us, to make disciples, and that starts with sharing Jesus, to a lost and dying world. May the Lord bless you in your efforts to win souls for Jesus' kingdom.

Matthew 28:19-20

[19] Go therefore and make disciples of all the nations, baptizing them in the name of the Father and of the Son and of the Holy Spirit, [20] teaching them to observe all things that I have commanded you; and lo, I am with you always, *even* to the end of the age." Amen.

So, getting back to this delusion that "it's about love" let me summarize that without love for God first there isn't any real, true, and lasting love. It starts there, with God, and then the Lord gives us the ability to reach out to love others, through and in Christ. That kind of love will then be pure, without the influences associated with the physical, or sexual desires of the flesh.

When the LGBT community speaks of love it's not the love God expects from us to provide to that community. Acceptance, affirmation, and/or political correctness, are not the appropriate responses, or approach, for a Christian to have on this issue. If we truly love them, we need to start with the truth, the truth God has given us, which is that they must turn from their sin, or face the consequences of eternal damnation. The message must be delivered with compassion, but we truly can't take any other stand.

In the book of John, Jesus did state that if we truly love Him, we would keep His word.

John 14:23-24
[23] Jesus answered and said to him, "If anyone loves Me, he will keep My word; and My Father will love him, and We will come to him and make Our home

with him. [24] He who does not love Me does not keep My words; and the word which you hear is not Mine but the Father's who sent Me.

God's word tells us to share the gospel of repentance with sinners for the remission of sin with a dying world. No excuses, no hesitation, no distractions, and no acceptance of the world's philosophy, or thinking, should deter us from that calling.

Please pray for boldness for me, and yourself, as we share the love of Christ the way He intended.

1 John 2:4
He who says, "I know Him," and does not keep His commandments, is a liar, and the truth is not in him.

Chances are if you do it the way Jesus instructed, you will not be accepted, and your family may be divided. Jesus told us that would occur in the scriptures.

Luke 12:51-53
[51] Do *you* suppose that I came to give peace on earth? I tell you, not at all, but rather division. [52] For from now on five in one house will be divided: three against two, and two against three. [53] Father will be divided against son and son against father, mother against daughter and daughter against mother, mother-in-law against her daughter-in-law and daughter-in-law against her mother-in-law."

The great thing is that there is a light at the end of the tunnel for those that persevere, eternal life.

<u>Matthew 19:29</u>
And everyone who has left houses or brothers or sisters or father or mother or wife or children or lands, for My name's sake, shall receive a hundredfold, and inherit eternal life.

Let's not lose sight of the prize. We are here for a short time compared to eternity, so let's take with us, as many as we can, by sharing our Lord and Savior Jesus Christ.

Scriptures to consider when seeking to identify with the Love of God and Jesus Christ:

Psalm 31:23
Oh, love the Lord, all you His saints! *For* the Lord preserves the faithful, And fully repays the proud person.

Psalm 70:4
Let all those who seek You rejoice and be glad in You; And let those who love Your salvation say continually, "Let God be magnified!"

Proverbs 8:17
I love those who love me, And those who seek me diligently will find me.

John 14:21
He who has My commandments and keeps them, it is he who loves Me. And he who loves Me will be loved by My Father, and I will love him and manifest Myself to him."

1 Corinthians 8:3
But if anyone loves God, this one is known by Him.

1 Corinthians 16:22
If anyone does not love the Lord Jesus Christ, let him be accursed. O Lord, come!

2 Timothy 2:22
Flee also youthful lusts; but pursue righteousness, faith, love, peace with those who call on the Lord out of a pure heart.

Hebrews 12:6
For whom the Lord loves He chastens, And scourges every son whom He receives."

1 Peter 4:8
And above all things have fervent love for one another, for "love will cover a multitude of sins."

Revelation 3:19
As many as I love, I rebuke and chasten. Therefore be zealous and repent.

Psalm 9:8

He shall judge the world in righteousness, And He shall administer judgment for the peoples in uprightness.

Delusion #3 - Don't Judge

The third delusion is the one that I hear most often, from people that have been twisted into a knot, because the enemy has misappropriated God's word about judging. The Christian community has gotten confused on what it means, and some, possibly many, are unable to discern God's word on this subject.

I've often heard from Christian's that we are not to judge people professing to be gay, lesbian, etc., but what does God really say about judging? Do we have a misunderstanding of what God says in His word, and have therefore become accepting of sinful behavior?

The enemy is deceitful and has taken words such as judge, judging, and judgement, and used them to shame Christian's from sharing God's truth. When we state that same sex relationships are sinful, as well as other LGBT sins, the words judge, and judging, are used against us to mean bigoted or hateful. This shift has confused many, and hindered our ability to use discernment when it comes to sin, or sinful behavior, and silenced us from sharing truth.

In looking at God's word let's look at the first time Satan used deceit as a weapon. In Genesis 3:2 where the serpent said to Eve "Has God indeed said," questioning, and placing doubt in her mind about what God said, and tempting her to sin.

Satan also used the same strategy to tempt Jesus by using God's word, and twisting it to suit his evil motives. Let's first look at what's in Psalm 91 and we'll compare it to what was quoted to Jesus by Satan in Matthew, where I've underlined the identical words used.

Psalm 91:11
[1] For <u>He shall give His angels charge over you,</u>
To keep you in all your ways.
[12] In *their* hands they shall bear you up,
Lest you dash your foot against a stone.

Matthew 4:6
[6] and said to Him, "If You are the Son of God, throw Yourself down. For it is written:

'<u>He shall give His angels charge over you,</u>

In the Psalm when those words are used it is to place our trust in God, but Satan uses it in Matthew to put God to a test. Jesus replied.

Matthew 4:7
[7] Jesus said to him, "It is written again, 'You shall not tempt the LORD your God.'

Jesus knew that we should never tempt, or in other words, put God to a test.

In the book of James, we read that God is beyond temptation by evil. In addition, God does not tempt us, so we can never say that when we sin, or fall into temptation, that God was in any way to blame for our failures.

James 1:13
Let no one say when he is tempted, "I am tempted by God"; for God cannot be tempted by evil, nor does He Himself tempt anyone.

So, let's look at a scripture often referred to around judging others and see what it says.

Matthew 7:1-4
"Judge not, that you be not judged. For with what judgment you judge, you will be judged; and with the measure you use, it will be measured back to you. And why do you look at the speck in your brother's eye, but do not consider the plank in your own eye?

These verses are giving a very specific reason for not judging. If we judge someone, and have sin in our lives that requires our attention, then we should consider our own sin before judging that of others.

This is intended to keep all of us in line, and teach us not to condemn, and it is to help in the process of bringing others towards salvation. If we approach someone in sin it shouldn't be accusatory, but in humility knowing that the Lord can forgive, and we should also have forgiveness in our hearts.

Note that Jesus continued with the following:

Matthew 7:5
[5] Hypocrite! First remove the plank from your own eye, and then you will see clearly to remove the speck from your brother's eye.

He wants us to be sure we know our lives are right with Him before we approach anyone in a self-righteous manner. There's a warning also at the end of those verses where Jesus tells them the following:

Matthew 7:16
[6] "Do not give what is holy to the dogs; nor cast your pearls before swine, lest they trample them under their feet, and turn and tear you in pieces.

When Jesus said the above, it was a warning that if, and when, it becomes obvious the gospel is not welcomed, and is just being trampled on, we're to move on, and find others who are ready to listen.

We are still required to share the gospel, not just think, decide, or say, "Well I'm not going to tell them about Jesus, and His plan for salvation, because they'll think I'm judging them." The plan of salvation also includes repentance of sin, and then following Christ. If they reject the message of salvation, they have made their choice, and we have done our part to reach the lost.

Our primary goal in telling people about Jesus is to bring them to His saving grace. The decision, to accept, or deny, Jesus as their savior, as it has always been, is theirs. We can't decide for others, and ultimately, we can't save anyone, only Christ can do that, and it's based on their decision to accept, or reject, Him.

Judgment will eventually be done by the Lord just as He has done throughout history. Notice that when Jesus came, He also told us that judgment was committed, or given to Him. Judgment will be performed by Jesus.

John 5:22-23
[22] For the Father judges no one, but has committed all judgment to the Son, [23] that all should honor the Son just as they honor the Father. He who does not honor the Son does not honor the Father who sent Him.

Jesus continues a few verses later with the following:

John 5:27
[27] and has given Him authority to execute judgment also, because He is the Son of Man.

Then Jesus follows that with another statement that clarifies that He, Jesus, does not seek His own will, and judges based on the will of the Lord, His Father.

John 5:30
[30] I can of Myself do nothing. As I hear, I judge; and My judgment is righteous, because I do not seek My own will but the will of the Father who sent Me.

We must remember that Jesus has made it clear in scripture that He and the Father are one.

John 10:30
I and *My* Father are one.

Jesus also made it clear that if we love Him, we keep His word, and His word is not His, but the Father's because they are **one**.

John 14:23-24
[23] Jesus answered and said to him, "If anyone loves Me, he will keep My word; and My Father will love him, and We will come to him and make Our home with him. [24] He who does not love Me does not keep My words; and the word which you hear is not Mine but the Father's who sent Me.

Scripture tells us the Lord has judged, and will continue to judge. It also tells us his judgment is true and righteous.

Psalm 19:9
The fear of the Lord *is* clean, enduring forever;
The judgments of the Lord *are* true *and* righteous altogether.

Psalm 7:11
God *is* a just judge, And God is angry *with the wicked* every day.

In the Old Testament, the Lord tells His people that it would be well for them, and their days would be prolonged in their land, when they walk in all the ways He has commanded.

Deuteronomy 5:33
You shall walk in all the ways which the Lord your God has commanded you, that you may live and *that it may be* well with you, and *that* you may

prolong *your* days in the land which you shall possess.

I'm seeing a division across our land, and wondering how long it will be before we will lose possession of our land and our freedoms. We are getting further from the Lord and walking in darkness. Only one way to correct course and that is to walk in the light of Jesus.

1 John 1:6-7
If we say that we have fellowship with Him, and walk in darkness, we lie and do not practice the truth. [7] But if we walk in the light as He is in the light, we have fellowship with one another, and the blood of Jesus Christ His Son cleanses us from all sin.

Let's now look at what happened throughout the history of Israel when they walked away or rejected the Lord.

Numbers 14:23
they certainly shall not see the land of which I swore to their fathers, nor shall any of those who rejected Me see it.

2 Kings 17:20
And the Lord rejected all the descendants of Israel, afflicted them, and delivered them into the hand of plunderers, until He had cast them from His sight.

In the New Testament, Jesus was clear in defining what rejection of Him meant. It was clear that by rejecting Him we were rejecting His Father, the Lord. But let's not lose sight that Jesus was telling his disciples, that if they were rejected, that was the same as rejecting Jesus, which also meant they were rejecting God the Father.

Luke 10:16

He who hears you hears Me, he who rejects you rejects Me, and he who rejects Me rejects Him who sent Me."

Scripture tells us to not be conformed to this world. We must not follow the path of others around us because we want to, "go along, to get along." The Lord wants us to walk in peace, but that does not mean to be like the world, and compromise His word. Please believe me, I hate confrontation, and I'm not the guy that will argue a point because I get flustered. But I am called to make the point that Jesus is the way, the truth, and the light, and that salvation is only through Him.

Romans 12:2

And do not be conformed to this world, but be transformed by the renewing of your mind, that you may prove what *is* that good and acceptable and perfect will of God.

The Christian community has become divided because we are not staying in God's word. We are being led astray by every new whim that comes along and tickles our ears. Why? The word tells us that it's because of rebellion. Our society has rebelled against the Lord and as long as it continues in that path, we will see more division and greater challenges.

Ezekiel 12:2
"Son of man, you dwell in the midst of a rebellious house, which has eyes to see but does not see, and ears to hear but does not hear; for they *are* a rebellious house.

There are churches accepting sin within their walls. While scripture does tell us to love people, but as I mentioned in a previous chapter, we first need to love the Lord above all else, before we can do the latter. Accepting sin in the midst of the church is not love, but rebellion, and is very divisive.

Luke 11:17
But He, knowing their thoughts, said to them: "Every kingdom divided against itself is brought to desolation, and a house *divided* against a house falls.

Mark 3:24:25
If a kingdom is divided against itself, that kingdom cannot stand. [25] And if a house is divided against itself, that house cannot stand.

It's also interesting to me that scripture tells us to discipline a brother, or fellow Christian, in the church, and yet we stop short of that because we don't want to judge anyone. We have lost our ability to discern, and take action that's necessary to correct false or misleading teachings. We should never allow someone who is openly living in sin, and an unrepentant life, to stay in the church.

1 Corinthians 5:11-13
[11] But now I have written to you not to keep company with anyone named a brother, who is sexually immoral, or covetous, or an idolater, or a reviler, or a drunkard, or an extortioner—not even to eat with such a person. [12] For what *have* I *to do* with judging those also who are outside? Do you not judge those who are inside? [13] But those who are outside God judges. Therefore "put away from yourselves the evil person."

How much clearer do we need to be to see that we have the authority of God's word, that tells us to judge within the church, and God judges those outside.

In the next chapter of 1 Corinthians the apostle Paul goes further by telling us that the saints, that's us, those that have been saved by Jesus Christ, will judge the world and also judge angels.

1 Corinthians 6:2-3
[2] Do you not know that the saints will judge the world? And if the world will be judged by you, are you unworthy to judge the smallest matters? [3] Do you not know that we shall judge angels? How much more, things that pertain to this life?

The above scripture makes it clear by asking a rhetorical question, which tells us that the saints, Christians, will judge the world. Then Paul goes on to also ask, "are you unworthy to judge the smallest matters?" If we can't do the little things, or the smallest things in this world, how will the Lord trust us to judge the bigger things? In addition, he goes on to tell us a mystery, through another rhetorical question, that we shall judge angels.

When I hear a Christian say we are not to judge, that tells me they do not understand God's word, are spiritually immature, or are still babe's in the knowledge of the Lord. The only other option left, if none of those three apply, is that they have compromised God's word.

Let's look at what God's word tells us about our level of maturity and where we should be once we've been following His word over a period of time and study.

Hebrews 5:12:13
For though by this time you ought to be teachers, you need *someone* to teach you again the first principles of the oracles of God; and you have come to need milk and not solid food. [13] For everyone who partakes *only* of milk *is* unskilled in the word of righteousness, for he is a babe.

There have been times when I've tried to correct someone's thinking, but it has rarely gone well. They are convinced we shouldn't judge, and have lost their ability to be discerning. I don't get into arguments with people making such statements, or about their misunderstanding of God's word because I believe they have not been properly taught, and have also made up their minds on this matter.

In some cases, I've been unprepared to have that conversation at the time. Sometimes it has been at an inopportune time, such as in a public place, during a dinner, or a night out. In other cases, it has occurred during a casual conversation with someone I have just met, and the only thing I know about them is that they told me they are a Christian. I pray that the Lord starts to give me the words, and deal with me in those times, and give me boldness to rebuke, and correct, as His word teaches.

When I read the scriptures, I've come to realize that the people that sought out Christ were looking for something that they weren't getting from the religious leaders of their time. When they heard Jesus, they knew that He spoke truth, and somehow, His word pierced their hearts, minds, and soul, and made clear to them their sin, so they were open to receiving His teachings.

I've also realized that many times conversations turn confrontational because people are not prepared to hear the truth of God's word. But we are to give them the word even in those instances. It may seem at times that it didn't sink in, but God's word also tells us that His word will accomplish what He wants.

Isaiah 55:11
So shall My word be that goes forth from My mouth; It shall not return to Me void, But it shall accomplish what I please, And it shall prosper *in the thing* for which I sent it

I also want to be clear; I'm not advocating that we should cast out anyone from our churches that comes in with sin in their lives. We all came to Christ as sinners, and through the study of God's word, we came to the realization that we are sinners needing repentance to receive the salvation of the Lord. But without repentance there is no remission of sin.

Some may come back and say, Christ ate and visited with sinners. True, but what was the purpose of that?

Luke 5:32
I have not come to call *the* righteous, but sinners, to repentance."

Sinners came to Christ because they were seeking something that the religious leaders of their time could not give, or provide them. Jesus spoke and ate with sinners to bring them to His saving grace, giving them the opportunity to repent, and to follow Him. What a loving God we serve that He came to meet with us, where we are, to bring us to the knowledge of His saving grace and mercy.

Luke 15:1-2,10
[1] Then all the tax collectors and the sinners drew near to Him to hear Him. [2] And the Pharisees and scribes complained, saying, "This Man receives sinners and eats with them."
[10] Likewise, I say to you, there is joy in the presence of the angels of God over one sinner who repents."

I've covered much ground above so let me get back to my initial topic on judging. There have been significant attacks on the church creating much confusion that we, the saints, the sons of the kingdom, have been unable to discern that we are in the midst of a very sinister spiritual battle. The scriptures have been twisted to make us ineffective and to doubt God's word.

The constant bombardment with the question that was raised back in Genesis, "did God really say" is being played out in our world today at an alarming, and increasing rate, and we have let our guard down by not staying focused on God's word and in prayer.

First, we have questioned, and doubted, our right, or ability to judge, especially within our churches. Then the world, non-believers, and what scriptures call tares, have crept into the church, and told us we are wrong to judge others by twisting God's word.

Some of our leaders have stopped giving us the full truth, for various reasons, but we, the body of Christ, have stopped holding them, and each other accountable to God's word. We have allowed our leaders to stray from God's word, and we, as the church, and body of Christ, have strayed away by our own desires, and while doing that false teachers, tares, and hirelings, have crept in.

The battle lines need to be drawn, and the church of Jesus Christ needs to rise up, and fight the spiritual battle that currently rages for the souls of those around us. We live in a dying, and decaying world,

so let's put on our armor and let's be engaged in the
battle to the glory of God.

Scriptures to consider while reflecting on the righteous Judge, the Lord:

Psalm 9:8
He shall judge the world in righteousness, And He shall administer judgment for the peoples in uprightness.

Psalm 50:6
Let the heavens declare His righteousness, For God Himself *is* Judge.

Psalm 51:4
Against You, You only, have I sinned, And done *this* evil in Your sight— That You may be found just when You speak, *And* blameless when You judge.

Ecclesiastes 3:17
I said in my heart, "God shall judge the righteous and the wicked, For *there is* a time there for every purpose and for every work."

Isaiah 66:16
For by fire and by His sword The Lord will judge all flesh; And the slain of the Lord shall be many.

Ezekiel 34:22
therefore I will save My flock, and they shall no longer be a prey; and I will judge between sheep and sheep.

Acts 17:30-31

[30] Truly, these times of ignorance God overlooked, but now commands all men everywhere to repent, [31] because He has appointed a day on which He will judge the world in righteousness by the Man whom He has ordained. He has given assurance of this to all by raising Him from the dead."

2 Timothy 4:8

Finally, there is laid up for me the crown of righteousness, which the Lord, the righteous Judge, will give to me on that Day, and not to me only but also to all who have loved His appearing.

Hebrews 10:30

For we know Him who said, "Vengeance is Mine, I will repay," says the Lord. And again, "The Lord will judge His people."

Revelation 20:11-13

[11] Then I saw a great white throne and Him who sat on it, from whose face the earth and the heaven fled away. And there was found no place for them. [12] And I saw the dead, small and great, standing before [a]God, and books were opened. And another book was opened, which is *the Book* of Life. And the dead were judged according to their works, by the things which were written in the books. [13] The sea gave up the dead who were in it, and Death and Hades delivered up the dead who were in them. And they were judged, each one

according to his works.

Matthew 15:14

Let them alone. They are blind leaders of the blind. And if the blind leads the blind, both will fall into a ditch."

Leaders, Saints, Tares, and Hirelings

As part of my journey I've often asked myself many questions regarding the church, its leaders, and the saints, otherwise known as Christians, or the body of Christ. Then there are the questions regarding the tares, those that are in the church but not truly saved, non-Christians, that bring in false doctrine and teachings. Since my focus has been to find God's truth, I feel the need to also look at addressing the four areas above, which primarily makeup, and are the essence of the modern-day church.

In my quest, I've primarily looked at the New Testament books to get clarity. The first four books, are referred to as the gospels, and tell the history of Jesus, coming as the Lord and Savior of mankind. Those books are followed by the book of Acts, which show Jesus at work as He continues to act, through his apostles, and the Holy Spirit. The rest of the books, or letters, were written to the saints, as well as leaders, of the church to provide guidance, structure and to teach us to guard against false teachers, that crept, and continue to creep, into the church.

So, let's go over the first two characters written to in the letters of scripture which are the leaders, and the saints, and address the many questions I've had of each. I'll start with a look at what Paul told Timothy about church leaders, (bishop or overseer), and their qualifications.

1 Timothy 3:1-7

This *is* a faithful saying: If a man desires the position of a bishop, he desires a good work. [2] A bishop then must be blameless, the husband of one wife, temperate, sober-minded, of good behavior, hospitable, able to teach; [3] not given to wine, not violent, not greedy for money, but gentle, not quarrelsome, not covetous; [4] one who rules his own house well, having *his* children in submission with all reverence [5] (for if a man does not know how to rule his own house, how will he take care of the church of God?); [6] not a novice, lest being puffed up with pride he fall into the *same* condemnation as the devil. [7] Moreover he must have a good testimony among those who are outside, lest he fall into reproach and the snare of the devil.

That's quite a list of qualifications. So, when I look at this list, I realize that our leaders are just men, seeking God's will, to do the work that the Lord has placed in their hearts and lives. On the other hand, I believe that if a church leader is truly seeking God's will they will be able to meet, and live up to those qualifications, with God's leading through His Holy Spirit. By my statement I don't mean that they will do this perfectly, they may falter, and even fail at times, but be able to get beyond those moments, by abiding, or staying connected to, our Lord Jesus.

John 15:5

"I am the vine, you *are* the branches. He who abides in Me, and I in him, bears much fruit; for without Me you can do nothing.

So, below are some of the questions that I've had for, and regarding, church pastors and leaders. While they are in no particular order, or importance, these have been on my mind, and maybe on yours as well.

- Are our church leaders and pastors staying true to God's word?
- Have our leaders failed, our brothers and sisters in the Lord, when we, the saints, can't discern truth, from heresy, and false teachings?
- Is the message of the gospel being taught with the full assurance, and authority, that is given to believers as the children, sons and daughters, of the living God?
- Have our leaders watered down the message of the gospel to satisfy the masses, and those in our midst that are the tares, the weeds, that are sitting among the wheat, the children of the living God?

Then there are other questions regarding those that may have questionable qualifications. Maybe qualifications is not the right word, maybe the word, calling, is more appropriate, but I feel this particular word is often misused. There are many qualified, having studied, and receiving the credentials from accredited schools, but maybe it's more around their ability to lead based on their leading from God.

Yes, I've seen many leaders that are loving, and caring, but are they the leaders we need in an age where God's authority is questioned at every turn?

Yes, they know the scriptures, but are they so grounded in God's word, that the Holy Spirit leads them in the battle, to face the attacks of the current culture? Are some of our church leaders truly prepared to lead? I'm not just talking about schooling, or institutionalized learning, but learning from the Lord, in His word, and at His feet.

I've seen some great pastors, and leaders, speak God's word in truth. Many can fully defend the gospel, but in our current culture, the truth of God's word, to those opposing God's word, doesn't matter. Do we continue to engage those opposing us, and God's word, in their battlefield, and with the same weapon's the world uses?

We are fighting a spiritual battle, using God's word, on nonbelievers, who do not want to understand, or cannot relate to His word, and in many instances are openly opposed to it. Many in our culture have been, what I'll call, inoculated, against God's word by demonic forces because they are children of the devil. I've quoted this scripture before, but it's worth repeating, when Jesus said as much to the Pharisees, the religious rulers, of His time.

John 8:44
You are of *your* father the devil, and the desires of your father you want to do. He was a murderer from the beginning, and does not stand in the truth, because there is no truth in him. When he speaks a lie, he speaks from his own *resources,* for he is a liar and the father of it.

So, my next question is do we continue to fight a spiritual battle without fully understanding the battlefield and our opponents? Knowing this is a spiritual battle requires us to use our full armor, which I presented at the beginning of this book, and will discuss again later.

An unfortunate thing that I've seen is that some church leaders have stopped delivering the truth of the gospel and have watered-down the message. I've seen a dependency on the approval, or acceptance, of their church members, and not on the Lord, and it has weakened them from speaking the truth.

Leaders who are worried that the people will leave, and impact them personally, need to remember that God is bigger than any of that. If the people in the church can't handle God's truth, how will they stand when persecution comes, or on the day of God's judgement?

The most unfortunate thing is that there are also false teachers leading the church today. They make a mockery of God's word by bringing in false doctrine and heresies. Many people can't, or won't, discern the truth because they have not sought God's word diligently for knowledge. Their own relationship with Jesus Christ has little, or no depth, or is nonexistent.

2 Peter 2:1
But there were also false prophets among the people, even as there will be false teachers among you, who will secretly bring in destructive heresies,

even denying the Lord who bought them, *and* bring on themselves swift destruction.

2 Peter 3:17-18
You therefore, beloved, since you know *this* beforehand, beware lest you also fall from your own steadfastness, being led away with the error of the wicked; [18] but grow in the grace and knowledge of our Lord and Savior Jesus Christ.

As Peter warned the people, he was also very clear to not allow themselves to be, "led away with the error of the wicked." We live in a world full of teachings that are contrary to God's word, and there should be no doubt in a Christian's mind, that when a leader's teachings deviates from God's word, we are not to accept it just because it comes from someone who professes to speak for the Lord. If you hear false teachings in your church, correct it, using God's word, and if it's rejected by the leaders, flee that church, and find one that teaches God's word.

The second set of characters that the New Testament addresses are the saints, the body of Christ, which is just as important, if not more important, and relevant, and which I believe needs a course correction. Some of the questions below I've asked have been around the lack of fervor, enthusiasm, and desire, to seek and learn from God's word.

• Where is the zeal, and love for God?

- Are we seeking Him with all our hearts, mind, soul and strength?
- Why are people in our churches, the saints, confused on some of the clear teachings of scripture?
- Where is discipleship in our churches?
- Why are so many women alone in the church, and more importantly, where are the men?
- Why is our commitment to the Lord so shallow?

One thing I've noticed in particular is that it is a rare thing for there to be discipleship in the church. The first 15 plus years, after I was saved, I had never heard of discipleship. Yes, there has usually been Sunday school, but those classes are primarily intended to teach specific things on God's word. What is needed is mentoring, coaching, instruction and accountability in the application of God's word. We need to know how to apply God's word in practical ways, and used in our daily lives that will impact our lives, and the life of others.

After many years I've realized that discipleship is much more important to the growth, and maturity, of a Christian's faith, and walk with the Lord, than sitting in a class and getting information. While it is good information, many of us in this culture don't know how, or understand the ways, to apply the teachings. I believe that discipleship would address the bigger problem which is that we don't feel fully assured that God's word is truth, and feel ill equipped, and lack the confidence to defend it.

I've also seen that there are many excuses each of us make to not seek, or devote time to learning, and understanding, God's word. In my 30 plus years as a Christian, I've attended primarily small churches, and I've heard many excuses, and made many of them myself, for not finding time to devote to learning God's word. Unfortunately, there is another aspect, many saints have little interest in pursuing the deeper things offered by the church. The busyness of life often takes us away from going into a deeper relationship with the Lord.

But to be honest I believe some of it is simply just laziness. We go to church, and often hear a message that will make us feel better about life, and leave without truly spending time in the Lord's presence, and engaging Him in our lives.

Please don't get me wrong I've been guilty of being too busy to pursue God's word. When the kids were young, we were engaged in activities with, and for, them that drew us away. At other times there were other activities, or functions, I had an interest in attending. Then there were the excuses, such as the class, or lesson, was being held too late, or too early, for me to attend. Our priorities are often not aligned with what needs to occur to fully develop our relationship with Christ.

In addition, we have Christian's that are not interested in pursuing and growing in God's word. The world has a strong hold on many of us today. When I say us, I have to include myself because to my shame I have often fallen into habits, and sin,

118

that I know are not pleasing to the Lord. The one thing that I have learned is that no matter how many times I've read God's word, the Bible, the more I realize that I've only touched the surface of what it has to say to me.

Let's take a look at a parable that Jesus shared with His disciples in the book of Matthew. In this case, a man, planted good seed, and yet among the seed an enemy planted "tares," which is a weed that looks much like wheat in its early stages of growth. The man told them to let them grow together, and when the harvest comes, or the day of judgement, they will gather and burn the tares.

Matthew 13:24-30
[24] Another parable He put forth to them, saying: "The kingdom of heaven is like a man who sowed good seed in his field; [25] but while men slept, his enemy came and sowed tares among the wheat and went his way.[26] But when the grain had sprouted and produced a crop, then the tares also appeared. [27] So the servants of the owner came and said to him, 'Sir, did you not sow good seed in your field? How then does it have tares?' [28] He said to them, 'An enemy has done this.' The servants said to him, 'Do you want us then to go and gather them up?' [29] But he said, 'No, lest while you gather up the tares you also uproot the wheat with them. [30] Let both grow together until the harvest, and at the time of harvest I will say to the reapers, "First gather together the tares and bind them in bundles to burn them, but gather the wheat into my barn." ' "

When Jesus explained the parable to His disciples, he clarified what it meant. The "man" was Jesus, who also referred to Himself, as the "Son of Man." The enemy was clearly the devil. The wheat refers to us, His children, the tares are sons of the devil, and they are in our midst.

Matthew 13:37-39

[37] He answered and said to them: "He who sows the good seed is the Son of Man. [38] The field is the world, the good seeds are the sons of the kingdom, but the tares are the sons of the wicked *one*. [39] The enemy who sowed them is the devil, the harvest is the end of the age, and the reapers are the angels.

Please note that tares, or weeds, was used by Jesus only in the book of Matthew. There are people sitting in our churches that are not sons of the kingdom. They are not focused on following God's word, and have not been transformed to reflect His image, or living a life that points to Him. They have much of the world in them that reflects their father, the devil. All that we can do about that is to continue to pray that the Lord, through His Holy Spirit, will truly open their hearts to Him.

Another thing that I see in the church is that there are those that are not called to preach the gospel, but see this as a career. Jesus referred to them in the book of John.

John 10:12-14

[12] But a hireling, *he who is* not the shepherd, one who does not own the sheep, sees the wolf coming and leaves the sheep and flees; and the wolf catches

the sheep and scatters them. [13] The hireling flees because he is a hireling and does not care about the sheep. [14] I am the good shepherd; and I know My *sheep,* and am known by My own.

Are we, as children of God, unable to discern those that are hirelings? The New Testament church had its challenges with false teachers, and we see many examples of that given by Paul, Peter, John, and other disciples, warning the churches that they ministered to, about false teachings, and instructing them to stay focused on God's word to combat those that had crept into the church.

These tares, false teachers, or hirelings, currently in our churches, are destroying the church from within. They say the right things such as "I'll pray for you" or "God is good' but they are not truly following Jesus Christ as presented in the gospels. Some in the church have created a God in their own image, they are idolaters.

While they speak the language, the church has become accustomed to, which I've often heard referred to as Christianese, they have created a God that tolerates all, disciplines none, sin is no longer an issue, and grace covers it all. God is love, but the word is clear that without repentance, there is no remission of sin. God's grace does not excuse sin.

1 John 1:8-10
[8] If we say that we have no sin, we deceive ourselves, and the truth is not in us. [9] If we confess our sins, He is faithful and just to forgive us *our* sins and to cleanse us from all

unrighteousness. [10] If we say that we have not sinned, we make Him a liar, and His word is not in us.

I'm not looking to make everyone doubtful, and suspicious, or call into question each person, or move within the church. My desire is to wake us up, and call us to be discerning to what is going on around us. There are tares in the midst of the church, and false teachers, that are questioning the teachings on sin, especially sexual sin.

The church is portrayed, today, as the culprit for addressing sexual sin in a culture that has redefined sexuality. Redefining sexuality has given them the impetus to attack the Christian community, and what I've seen is that even good, and well-meaning, pastors, have been convinced that by loving, calling it grace, and allowing sin in their church, they are doing God's will.

A question I have for those pastors would be, have you compromised God's word to be inclusive? In addition, where did you get the idea, or how did you become convinced, that allowing sin was more loving, than warning them of the consequences of sin? An eternal question on my mind is, if the last minute they spent with you were their last, will you be fully convinced, and satisfied, with their eternal outcome?

The real love you need to show those in your church is to give them God's truth, and let Him work in their lives. Another question is when you look at the people sitting in your church are you able to deliver a message on sin as defined by God, or have you stopped short of delivering a message because of those sitting in the pews, and chairs, of your church?

So, after all these questions, and thoughts, about church leaders, the saints, tares, and hirelings, do I have any real solutions or answers? Is there another way, something better?

The church is not perfect, but it is what we have, and to give up on it, or not participate, is not an option I've ever considered. With all of its flaws, there are many in the church that seek, and love, the Lord, and are willing, and able, to help those that truly seek, and want Him.

The one thing I'd like to see added to every church is a discipleship program with it being a requirement, for a new believer, regular attender, or someone with the intent of membership. An elder, deacon, or mature believer, should be assigned for a period of time to ensure that the person is prepared to live a life that seeks, and knows the Lord. I know it's a lot to ask, especially since many in our churches are unwilling to serve, but when I look at Jesus' command to go to all the nations, He didn't say to make converts, He said to make disciples.

Matthew 28:19
Go therefore and make disciples of all the nations, baptizing them in the name of the Father and of the Son and of the Holy Spirit,

Yes, we must be about sharing the good news of the gospel, and the salvation offered by our Lord and Savior, Jesus Christ. But once a commitment is made, we must also provide discipleship.

Jesus spent three years with His disciples, and even with all His teachings, when confronted, and persecuted, they fled. The teachings He gave them helped them look to, and for, the promises He also made to them. Discipleship adds value that would help each saint look towards the promises the Lord has made, and gives us the strength to endure when trials, tribulations, and persecutions come.

In looking at the book of Revelations there is something that stands out to me for each church mentioned. There are seven churches mentioned, and except for Smyrna, the persecuted church, and the church of Philadelphia, which was known as the faithful church, five of them had at least one problem they needed to address, or to repent from. Yet all seven churches have a statement, and a promise, that followed at the end of the paragraph on the church.

The statement was to "him," or "he," who overcomes," there was a promise given. You see, the Lord our God, deals with each of us, one on one, in a personal relationship. We can attend, or be a part of, any one of those seven types of churches, the persecuted, the faithful, or those with flaws needing repentance, but ultimately, we'll all be held accountable for our own actions, not for what occurs, or does not occur, in the church.

In the scripture below God's word makes it clear that "He who overcomes," has God's promises of an inheritance, and our identity, as His children. Let's pursue the Lord and look to overcome in a world that has lost its way.

Revelations 21:6-7

6 And He said to me, "It is done! I am the Alpha and the Omega, the Beginning and the End. I will give of the fountain of the water of life freely to him who thirsts. **7 He who overcomes shall inherit all things, and I will be his God and he shall be My son.**

2 Peter 1:16

For we did not follow cunningly devised fables when we made known to you the power and coming of our Lord Jesus Christ, but were eyewitnesses of His majesty.

Fables, Fallacies and Fantasies

In looking at possible ways to describe this next chapter I chose the above words, because of the lunacy we are being subjected to, and how we've allowed ourselves to be silenced by attacks, and use of words, that are at best meaningless, and at worse evil. Our Lord warned us against the evil of the world, but we are now seeing evil at its extremes.

We see that many are turning from the truth because of the way they feel. As I wrote earlier some Christian's feel that people are born gay. They have turned aside to fables, in bold below for emphasize.

1 Timothy 1:4
[4] nor give heed to **fables** and endless genealogies, which cause disputes rather than godly edification which is in faith.

2 Timothy 4:3-4
[3] For the time will come when they will not endure sound doctrine, but according to their own desires, *because* they have itching ears, they will heap up for themselves teachers; [4] and they will turn *their* ears away from the truth, and be turned aside to **fables**.

In today's culture there are considerable accusations of Christian's being homophobic. What in the world does that mean? A phobia is an abnormal, irrational or obsessive fear, dread, terror, even hatred of something.

Think about it, do we Christian's fear a person that professes to be gay or lesbian? My answer is simply no, to fearing the person, or their lifestyle, but I am concerned about their eternal outcome. Love is the motivator for a true child of God, not hatred. Where there is hatred, that's not from God, but motivated by Satan.

2 Timothy 1:7
For God has not given us a spirit of fear, but of power and of love and of a sound mind.

In scripture there are more than 450 uses of the word fear. There are many reasons to be fearful but loving others, and wanting their salvation, is not a reason to fear. God's word tells us that we should not fear man, but to fear God, because although He is able to save, He is also able to cast people to hell.

Luke 12:4-5
4 "And I say to you, My friends, do not be afraid of those who kill the body, and after that have no more that they can do. 5 But I will show you whom you should fear: Fear Him who, after He has killed, has power to cast into hell; yes, I say to you, fear Him!

As far as hatred for them, that is just another lie which holds no water. My concern is their spiritual state, and the consequences of that state, which without salvation through Jesus Christ, is hell. Before my daughter's change in lifestyle, I must confess, I hadn't given a lot of thought to the spiritual state, and outcome, of those in that lifestyle. It's always interesting to me how the Lord gets our attention to things around us.

So, here is another question I have to ask. When two naked men stand side by side can you tell that one is supposedly gay? Two naked men, or two naked women, side by side will always be men or women, even to a blind man. Even the blind can touch, and feel the differences in their physical presence. There's much scientific biological evidence of only two sexes, yet it goes ignored. So why are we deceived? Simply put, it's because we don't believe God's word.

Let's look at this rationally. When do we normally discover, or find out, that one of two men, or one of two women, are gay or lesbian? Usually, when they either tell us, or in the case of the man when they make some gesture that suggest that one is effeminate. We have to be told, or we have to see, a sign from them. Their God given biological sex can be clearly seen for anyone to determine. They have decided to disbelieve what can be clearly seen. A fallacy at best, sin at its core.

I find phobias interesting because they are for the most part irrational. My greatest phobia is a fear of bugs. And you know what I've discovered, that when I see a cockroach, or a spider, I immediately recognize the cockroach, or spider, and react in fear. They never said a word, they just crawled into my line of sight. And my reaction is always pretty immediate, I run to get something to kill it with.

No such thing happens when I meet a man or woman. We can have a nice conversation, enjoy each other's company, and no reaction, except maybe, if they are dressed in a way that would reveal they believe themselves to be something other than a man or woman. In such a case, I would then react to the sin that they have in their lives. In my mind, someone dressing up as the opposite sex is just a fantasy of their own making.

Please don't tell me that we should not react to sin. We do it in all other circumstances. If we catch someone in a lie, stealing, or worse, murder, we react to the sin. The Lord gave us the ability of discernment, and the in the gospel of John, we need to recognize that the Lord placed in us an internal sin detector, our conscience.

John 8:9

Then those who heard *it,* being convicted by *their* conscience, went out one by one, beginning with the oldest *even* to the last. And Jesus was left alone, and the woman standing in the midst.

When did we start to question our ability to recognize sin? We can, and do recognize sin, and a great example was when Jesus said to those accusing the woman caught in adultery, "He who is without sin among you, let him throw a stone at her first." We often recognize the outward sin of others, but overlook the inward sin in ourselves, except as shown by our conscience.

The woman caught in sin wasn't excused from her sin, although it may appear that way. Each man recognized, via his own conscience, that they also were sinners, and could not convict her. But why didn't Jesus convict or condemn her? As Lord, He had every right to do so.

John 8:10-11
[10] When Jesus had raised Himself up and saw no one but the woman, He said to her, "Woman, where are those accusers of yours? Has no one condemned you?"
[11] She said, "No one, Lord."
And Jesus said to her, "Neither do I condemn you; go and sin no more."

The answer is so simple, yet profound. The woman recognized Him, Jesus, as Lord. Her recognition of Him as Lord was sufficient for Jesus to forgive her, but it was not an excuse for sin. It's important to note that He gave her instruction, in this case correction, to "go and sin no more." We can't take that lightly, since when Jesus forgives our sin there is a requirement based on His holy word, to sin no more.

Now we also must first recognize that we are all sinners. People that are not saved, or do not believe in Christ, do not believe they are sinners. In my own life I recognized after many failures that I was somehow a sinner, but I didn't know the full extent of sin until Jesus revealed it to me. We must also acknowledge that while we have these flawed human bodies we will fall into sin. The expectation by our Lord is for us, as his followers, to not fall into repetitive, and unrepentant sin.

Since being saved my goal has never been to stop sinning. Unfortunately, sin comes naturally. My true goal has been to know Jesus, and His word more, so that I recognize when I've sinned, or when I'm heading towards sin. The best I can ever do as a man, is to walk with Jesus, so that I'm never caught unawares, and when I sin, I recognize it. Yet, when I don't recognize it, or miss it, my hope and prayer is that when the Lord reveals it to me, I acknowledge it, and immediately repent.

I'm often reminded of King David, and his sin of adultery that led to murder. He didn't recognize the sin of adultery, and when faced with the prospect of being discovered, he committed another sin, murder, to cover up the first sin. It is significant to note what he said when he was confronted with his sin.

2 Samuel 12:13
13 So David said to Nathan, "I have sinned against the LORD." And Nathan said to David, "The LORD also has put away your sin; you shall not die.

David didn't say I sinned against man, by taking another man's wife, Bathsheba, and then arranging for Uriah, her husband's murder. Instantly, he recognized his sin was against God and the Lord spared his life. I often pray that we, the followers and children of God, seek and learn discernment. That our conscience would be so in tune to God's word that we would recognize our sin against the Lord, not when exposed, but before it comes to fruition, as it is conceived, and takes root in our mind and thoughts.

Why do I pray for discernment? Because based on scripture, and in particular the book of James, we see that sin, brings forth death. A spiritual death that we can't be rescued from, except through repentance, and following Jesus Christ.

James 1:15
Then, when desire has conceived, it gives birth to sin; and sin, when it is full-grown, brings forth death.

So, let's take note of what Nathan the prophet told David were the consequences of his sin.

2 Samuel 12:14-15
[14] However, because by this deed you have given great occasion to the enemies of the LORD to blaspheme, the child also *who is* born to you shall surely die." [15] Then Nathan departed to his house.

When we sin as a follower of Christ, we do give occasion to those looking at us a bad example, and it also gives them occasion to blaspheme. They don't believe that our God is real, they take His name in vain, because we have done a poor job of representing Him as ambassadors in this world.

You must understand there are always consequences to our sin, some outright for all to see, as in the scripture above, and some subtle, that only you might know or see. The woman caught in adultery faced a murderous mob, and was truly blessed that the Lord Jesus was on hand, otherwise she may have been stoned to death. The only thing that saved her was the grace and mercy of Jesus Christ.

The sexual sins of today are no different, the consequences are sometimes obvious, although maybe not to the sinner who denies God. Some, I pray, and believe will turn from their sin, and find a righteous, but very loving and merciful God. Others may not, and will find that there are consequences on the day of judgement. There are always consequences to sin, let's pray we can help many caught up in sexual sin, and the same sex lifestyle, before they must face the Lord.

In a recent conversation with a fellow believer, we were discussing how a church should handle, or address, a gay person, or couple, in church. By that I mean they are attending regularly, and claiming to be saved, but living a life that does not line up with God's word. This is a very compassionate sister in the Lord, and she expressed concerns that not allowing them to stay in the church was judgmental.

Her question to me was, if we cast them out, or condemn them, then how can we expect them to be saved? She emphasized that sanctification isn't immediate, and that if we don't give the Lord time to work in people's lives how will they ever come to salvation? She also added that Jesus wouldn't turn them away because they are sinners.

In another conversation, not long after, she used another reference of our salvation possibly helping that person to be saved. Although I understood her reference, that particular scripture was referring to the covenant relationship of a husband and wife which was established by God. I've included the scripture she was referring below:

1 Corinthians 7:16
[16] For how do you know, O wife, whether you will save *your* husband? Or how do you know, O husband, whether you will save *your* wife?

The scripture above only applies to a husband and wife relationship, and not intended to cover others outside of the marriage. And while I had to agree that Jesus is loving, and patient, He also calls sinners to repentance.

My answer to her goes back to my previous clarification where Jesus is calling sinners, and not the righteous to repentance (see the chapter on Delusion #2, It's about love). If they are in church, but don't think of themselves as sinners, are they being called, or are they simply the righteous, or tares, that don't see themselves as sinners in need of a savior?

Jesus loves us all and is very patient, and not willing that anyone perish, so He gives us time to repent. While that is true, my question to her was, when is the right time to confront the sinner, if there is no repentance? Just because a person claims to be a believer, while not living the life of a believer, are they truly a believer, are they saved? If they are not believers, although in words they claim to be, scripture tells us not to be unequally yoked with unbelievers.

2 Corinthians 6:14-15
[14] Do not be unequally yoked together with unbelievers. For what fellowship has righteousness with lawlessness? And what communion has light with darkness? [15] And what accord has Christ with Belial? Or what part has a believer with an unbeliever?

If we allow a gay person, or couples, in the church without confronting the sin in their lives, what about other sins? What happens with the adulterous man, or woman? When do we address the couple living together, but not married? What happens when we discover that a believer is cheating others in their business dealings? The list could go on and on.

In addition, how will our children react when we allow these things in a church, calling it sin, but unable to explain the contradiction? Will our children be able to grasp the concepts we try to teach them when we say one thing, but see another in the church? It is a slippery slope when we don't address sin in our midst.

Of course, this is a very delicate issue because we are there to reach the lost, but what if the sinner, or tares, in the church don't see themselves as lost? Sin, when clearly seen, or identified, needs to be addressed individually, in a case by case basis, and corporately, when necessary, in the church as the word is preached. If we don't, then the person can't ever go from their righteous state, (their belief that they are not sinners), to acknowledging they are sinners, in need of a savior.

When a person comes to Christ, we know that God deals with each of them as individuals, and where they are, when they come to Him for salvation. Some people have an immediate conversion while others are a work in progress. I don't have an answer, or formula, to address the sanctification process for each person, but do know that acceptance of the sin is not an option, because salvation requires repentance. Without repentance, there is no remission of sin, no salvation, and no heavenly outcome or reward. I've not been able to come up with a scenario that excuses sin, or makes it acceptable. Although I want to find a loop hole that would make everyone happy, it's just not there.

So, getting back to the phobia reference. Why do we shy away, and allow others to shut us up when accused of this so call "homophobia?" This is nonsense at its best, but let's follow this particular fantasy to its conclusion. Let's think about how most people with phobia's are treated. Usually there's compassion, or assistance, to help the person get over their fears.

There's no such thing available, or offered, to a so called, "homophobe." So, in reality this is a term used on Christian's to shut us up, and nothing more than a ploy to silence us from calling out sin for what it is. Let's not allow ourselves to get distracted by the devil's lies, and stand up for God's word in a culture that is lost, blind, and headed towards hell.

Let's also address the agenda of the LGBT movement because they have set out to label Christian's as hateful. They don't want to be called sinners so we have become the target of their hateful message. They have gained ground in making themselves appear the victim instead of being seen as sinners.

How did that happen? One aspect which I discussed earlier is that they have identified themselves with the labels used on them, making anything said against this sin a personal attack. But let's also think about what has been normalized since I've been alive. The culture and its messages have changed as part of the so-called sexual revolution. Below I've copied the definition of sexual revolution from Wikipedia.

The sexual revolution, also known as a time of sexual liberation, was a social movement that challenged traditional codes of behavior related to sexuality and interpersonal relationships throughout the United States and subsequently, the wider world, from the 1960s to the 1980s.[1] Sexual liberation included increased acceptance of sex outside of traditional heterosexual, monogamous relationships (primarily marriage). [2] The normalization of contraception and the pill, public nudity, pornography, premarital sex, homosexuality, masturbation, alternative forms of sexuality, and the legalization of abortion all followed.

Please note that this definition considers the sexual revolution as a time of sexual liberation, in other words freedom. It all boils down to a culture that has redefined sexual behavior and norms. In doing so, all kinds of sinful sexual behavior have been normalized because we have challenged the traditional behavior, that were at one time more aligned with God's word.

Sexual liberation brings about many desires which include wanting something outside of marriage. Before I was saved, I was divorced, and know all too well, how easy it was to leave my family, and move on with my life. When we want out of a marriage any excuse will do, but that is due to our sinful nature. Didn't make it right then, doesn't make it right today. But that's us as sinners, when we don't know Christ.

A man, or woman, who declares to know Christ and initiates divorce, doesn't truly know Christ. Just to clarify there are circumstances and situations, of abuse, that the Lord would not expect anyone to stay in, but for the most part the church is no different than the secular world in this area. We have gone the way of the world when it comes to marriage. Why? Because it's an easy "fix" instead of putting in the time, and effort, to work at, and save a marriage. In addition, our own desires lead us astray.

The deception in today's culture all goes back to the book of Genesis when the serpent asked Eve the question "has God indeed said." It all starts with questioning God's word, and in the case of sexual sin, the question becomes, did God really say marriage is between one man, and one woman? Satan's deceit is well at work in this day and age.

As far as sexual sin there doesn't seem to be an end in sight for its continued emphasis. The media plays a big part in delivering these sensual messages. It is very difficult to find a movie without a sexual scene, or message, and it doesn't matter that it adds nothing to the plot, it has to be there, after all it's entertaining, or is it? Make no mistake there is a message that is being clearly delivered to normalize sin even further in our culture.

The shows and movies have changed over the years, and the ratings no longer reflect a true picture of what we are seeing, or being exposed to. As I mentioned previously, in the last few years I've attempted to watch shows that are not "R," or "TV-MA," rated due to language, or sexual scenes, but even the lower ratings now have thrown in same sex relationships.

Most recently I was watching a series rated PG which should be appropriate for children with parental guidance. All seemed fine until episode 7, where they introduced two women together. The scene really had nothing to do with the plot, or story line, but it is the media trying to normalize same sex relationships, which is part of the LGBT agenda.

I've seen this take place in more shows than I care to mention, and each time I've stopped watching the movie or series. It doesn't matter that I'll not see the end of the movie, or series. What matters is what I'm saying to the Lord when I allow that in my home.

In addition, many companies in their commercials have given into the LGBT agenda with same sex couples thrown in, to continue to normalize this lifestyle. I find it offensive that this sin is being introduced into my home via the television, and you should be offended as well. I pray that I use my time in this world more appropriately than to sit and watch TV with its constant bombardment of sexual sin.

As part of my desire to see this turned around, I've actually started to follow, and participate with a Christian organization that often exposes, and fights to clean up movies and TV, and hold companies, and sponsors accountable. It is part of the American Family Association called "One Million Moms." You may want to poke fun at me since this was primarily established for women, but I will support any group that wants to push back, and hold the media and companies accountable, to ensure appropriate content for our children and grandchildren.

In addition, let's not forget pornography on demand via the internet to make things even more disturbing. How many of our friends, and neighbors, have become addicted to this medium, and making, or finding excuses for it, as if it's not a sin. The mind should also be dedicated to the Lord.

Romans 8:5-6
For those who live according to the flesh set their minds on the things of the flesh, but those *who live* according to the Spirit, the things of the Spirit. For to be carnally minded *is* death, but to be spiritually minded *is* life and peace.

As a nation when we allowed God to be taken out of the public schools, we delivered our children to a culture that does not revere, or fear God. Our children have been bombarded with sex education messages that are all outside of marriage. The messages to practice safe sex, and that same sex relationships are normal, have dominated our public-school system. Let's not be surprised when our children at some point in time are told that having sex with an adult is okay, or when the day comes that a pedophile starts visiting, and teaching openly at these schools.

Our children, in the public schools, have not been taught the implications of exercising sex outside of the way God intended, which is in marriage, between a man and a woman. Without God in the lives of our children, morality has become relative, and then the question that Pilate asked over twenty centuries ago when speaking to Jesus, have become all too common, "What is truth?"

If there are no standards, no real truth, for morality, then the question in everyone's mind is what do we believe? We believe what we are constantly told by the media, indoctrination, which we have made our source of information, and our god. We then start to believe that what's right for you, may not be what's right for me. With that thinking as the standard, anything goes, and we have opened the way for all kinds of possible sin. The interesting part is that we are seeing the exponential growth of sin due to the introduction of social media.

You can say anything you want, true or false, about anything, or anyone, and it goes out to hundreds, thousands, and millions in seconds. A society without a defined moral compass will lose it ways, and not recognize that they are blind, naked, and lost.

Another interesting thing to me is that with the internet, and social media, we have the technology that can actually capture Jesus' return for His people, and to judge the world. What I believe is that when this does occur, Jesus comes for His elect, many will not know what to believe since we're seeing such an abuse of the technology with fake news, lies, and deception.

Matthew 24:30-31

[30] Then the sign of the Son of Man will appear in heaven, and then all the tribes of the earth will mourn, and they will see the Son of Man coming on the clouds of heaven with power and great glory. [31] And He will send His angels with a great sound of a trumpet, and they will gather together His elect from the four winds, from one end of heaven to the other.

The Lord also warned us against getting into meaningless disputes. We often lose sight of what's truly worth discussing and get into arguments that lead nowhere. If something is clear in scripture why would a believer entertain, or take the side of, man's logic, or arguments?

We've allowed evolution to become the storyline in our schools to our children. Is evolution really science, or just a story? Are we to take man-made evolutionary theories seriously? At best this particular theory is a fantasy, which should be labeled science fiction. It is man using his creative mind, and telling us that there was a, "big bang," and that bang somehow, "miraculously'" created everything, including us. As a result, through billions and millions of years another "miracle" occurred and suddenly man came into being.

It's ironic that this "big bang" is considered a miracle by believers of evolution, but a God creating the universe could never have happened. There is no rational basis for this blind faith. There are many that will argue that the Bible is a story created by man. Then let's think about the source of the Bible, God.

2 Timothy 3:16
All Scripture *is* given by inspiration of God, and *is* profitable for doctrine, for reproof, for correction, for instruction in righteousness,

In addition, let's also realize that it was written over several centuries and decades, by more than 40 authors, proven historically accurate, consisting of 66 books, that talk about the same thing, one God, who sent His son, Jesus, to redeem us. Look at the scripture below, and instead of the name Timothy, replace it with yours, and let's stop those that profess knowledge from corrupting us, and let's stay faithful to our knowledge in the one true God.

1 Timothy 6:20-21
[20] O Timothy! Guard what was committed to your trust, avoiding the profane *and* idle babblings and contradictions of what is falsely called knowledge— [21] by professing it some have strayed concerning the faith.

Now let's take a look at another disturbing trend. Transgenders in our public libraries reading to our children. What parent in their right mind wants to expose their child to a man dressed in woman's apparel, and made up like a clown? This is no laughing matter these kids are being introduced to a demonic presence.

Please don't get me wrong these individual's need help, and much prayer, but not affirmation. They are dressed that way because they have a spiritual problem which in their sinful state they do not see. We, as children of God, need to be in prayer for their deliverance and salvation.

I also have to wonder why a mother, or father, would find this type of behavior from a man entertaining. In addition, from my perspective as a man, I would think a woman would find this offensive, that a man would portray them in such a manner. I would also ask the question, how did we, meaning men, get to such a low point, that we would value woman so little, that we would not defend the honor, and beauty, that God placed in the woman?

As I look back on my years, I've come to realize that the Lord placed the woman on this earth to provide man with much more than we have come to appreciate. Many times, as men, we tend to look at the outward appearance of the woman, and forget that she has a beauty beyond our senses. Women were meant by the Lord to complete us, our helper, but also comparable to us, which means so much more than we care to acknowledge.

Genesis 2:18
[18] And the LORD God said, "*It is* not good that man should be alone; I will make him a helper comparable to him."

Why are men struggling today with their identity, their jobs, being a husband, and/or a father? Simply put we've lost the biblical principles and foundation for a Godly family which includes a husband and wife. There is more value in our relationship with our wives than we care to admit, or acknowledge.

Proverbs 31 speaks about the virtuous wife, and below I've only copied three verses of that scripture, because it identifies her value to us men. In my mind, we have lost that knowledge, not only on the side of the men, but by the women as well.

Proverbs 31:10-12
[10] Who can find a virtuous wife?
For her worth *is* far above rubies.
[11] The heart of her husband safely trusts her;
So he will have no lack of gain.
[12] She does him good and not evil
All the days of her life.

If we don't find our way back to valuing each other, in a right relationship with the Lord, there really isn't a good way to fix what's broken in our society. We need the Lord more than ever to fight the spiritual battle that we are engaged in.

Colossians 1:9

For this reason we also, since the day we heard it, do not cease to pray for you, and to ask that you may be filled with the knowledge of His will in all wisdom and spiritual understanding;

The Spiritual Battle

This is a topic that probably will cause some controversy, or disagreement, but which I feel necessary to moving things forward. I've heard it many times, and by many pastors, as well as Christian radio, that we are in a spiritual battle. And while I agree, what does this really mean to the average person, and what does that really mean, in terms we can understand, act upon, and relate to?

The LGBT community I know thinks of us as intolerant, hateful, bigoted and other similar terms, but I'd like to think of a true follower of Jesus Christ as loving, and misunderstood, by our current culture. It's probably not practical to think that way, since we do disapprove of their lifestyle, but our goal is to bring them to the saving grace of Jesus Christ.

So, I'd like to break things down a little to things that are observable, and then discuss how we should be dealing with this issue.

Since my daughter started living this lifestyle, I've seen a transformation that tells me she's no longer the same person. On a physical level the changes she has made are obvious, and can be readily seen by anyone who knew her, before she turned to this lifestyle. To some extent I understand some of the changes, since she now has a new community that accepts, and encourages, her lifestyle choices.

The obvious physical changes that can be seen, or measured, are clearly a sign of things going on inside, which include changes to her character, personality, and more importantly to her soul. While we can't see the soul of someone, we are all influenced by what we believe, and accept, into our lives.

While she has become more assertive, and confident, those abilities existed in her before her lifestyle change. The lifestyle change became a catalyst, but it didn't have to be. The right type of support, and affirmation, from a Christian mentor, I believe, could have achieved the same results.

Another thing that I've come to realize is that it's hard for her to talk to us because I'm sure when she does it reminds her that we disapprove. It's also become obvious, that it's also hard for me to speak with her, because of the lifestyle she has chosen to live, which is in rebellion to God.

While I understand, I struggle that my daughter, who used to call regularly each week, now calls infrequently. Please note that we don't remind her that she's in sin, or that we disapprove of her lifestyle, since she already knows. So, the question then is, how does a person's personality change so completely, a change that impacts them physically and spiritually?

Let's look at this change based on my own experiences of going from living in the world, and then becoming a follower of Christ. When I was in the world, my thoughts were self-centered, primarily focused on what was right, or good, for me. Before salvation the questions I often asked were geared to address my needs, but most importantly my wants. How do I get what I need, or want, that will satisfy me, or make me happy?

Like most of us, I've had to work for a living, and previously lived according to the world, seeking success, and looking out for number one. I once was ambitious, and sought recognition, sometimes I still do, when focused on myself. I've read dozens of books on how to be successful in the business world, and for the most part the books primarily delivered self-centered messages. With the bombardment of these types of messages it's no wonder that our lives are so focused on self, and not others.

When I accepted Christ as Lord and Savior, I became focused on God's word, and my thoughts were transformed. The same thing happens in the other direction as well. When we walk away, or reject Christ, we are also transformed to be mindful of the things of this world.

Romans 12:2
And do not be conformed to this world, but be transformed by the renewing of your mind, that you may prove what *is* that good and acceptable and perfect will of God.

That transformation, for many of the children of Christian parents, can be clearly seen when they conform to the ways of the world. They do change, but it's a manifestation of what's occurred inside, to their inner being, because of the influences of demonic forces. When dealing with my daughter, I have to recognize that there is a battle for her soul.

So, I'm going to take us back to where I started in this book, when we looked at the book of Ephesians and to the following scripture:

Ephesians 6:12
12 For we do not wrestle against flesh and blood, but against principalities, against powers, against the rulers of the darkness of this age, against spiritual *hosts* of wickedness in the heavenly *places*.

The battle we are fighting is raging outside of our earthly realm, that is why scripture tells us to put on "the whole armor of God," that you may be able to "withstand." All the components, all the parts of the armor, must come together and be used as we have been instructed.

Ephesians 6:13-18
13 Therefore take up the whole armor of God, that you may be able to withstand in the evil day, and having done all, to stand.
14 Stand therefore, having girded your waist with truth, having put on the breastplate of righteousness, 15 and having shod your feet with the preparation of the gospel of peace; 16 above all, taking the shield of faith with which you will be able to quench all the fiery darts of the wicked one. 17 And take the helmet of salvation, and the sword of the Spirit, which is the word of God; 18 praying always with all prayer and supplication in the Spirit, being watchful to this end

with all perseverance and supplication for all the saints

The only way we'll be able to stand against the attacks of the enemy is with the full armor. Nothing else is sufficient, nothing else will do. So, gird your waist with truth, God's truth, put on the breastplate of righteousness, God's righteousness, shod your feet with the preparation of the gospel, use the shield of faith, and put on the helmet of salvation in Christ, **and then use the sword of the Spirit, which is the word of God.**

We can't take for granted any part of the armor. We must be grounded and stand in truth, in the righteousness of our Lord, and prepared with the gospel, in faith, in and through our salvation in Christ, and in the word of God.

Sometimes, I feel like a failure because some part, or piece of my armor, has been lacking, or misplaced. Primarily it has been because I've not spent enough time in God's word, and prayer, to feel prepared. Unfortunately, it's usually too easy to compromise, and our armor losses it's luster, as well as its strength.

We are told to pray for our children, but when the book of Ephesians above tells us to pray, it is in the power of God's might. Prayer in this battle requires the full armor to be used. In verse 18, we see that we are to pray in the Spirit, which is the Holy Spirit, living in us. We are neglecting the power of our Lord's might, if we simply pray in this battle without doing all prayer, and supplication, in the Spirit.

In the verses that followed Paul finished by asking the Christian's in Ephesus, to pray for him, that he would also be able to open his mouth boldly to make known the mystery of the gospel.

Ephesians 6:19-20
[19] and for me, that utterance may be given to me, that I may open my mouth boldly to make known the mystery of the gospel, [20] for which I am an ambassador in chains; that in it I may speak boldly, as I ought to speak.

Paul realized that he needed others to lift him up in prayer to speak boldly. It is no secret that our children, family members, and friends, need prayer while living in this lifestyle. But prayer needs to be made in faith, and not just wishful thinking.

I'm concerned that today we pray because that's the thing to do when someone is hurting, sick, in trouble, stressed, or in sin. The question we must ask ourselves is, do we truly believe that the Lord will show up and deliver a mighty work that we have not seen before? If we do, let's not grow weary.

Galatians 6:9
And let us not grow weary while doing good, for in due season we shall reap if we do not lose heart.

I'm reminded of the confrontation between Jesus and the Pharisees. He didn't mince words in telling them the truth. We have stopped telling others the truth with the conviction, and power, of the Holy Spirit.

I've gone over **John 8:44** previously, where Jesus was very clear in telling the Pharisees they were children of the devil. It's interesting as we read further down to verse **John 8:47** Jesus tells them, [47] He who is of God hears God's words; therefore you do not hear, because you are not of God."

The people who heard those words were not of God, and could not hear, or understand, what Jesus was trying to explain. That's the same situation we find ourselves in this day and age. The people do not understand us because they are of their father the devil. Our only recourse is to pray to our Heavenly Father for His guidance, and wisdom, as we face the forces of evil in this day and age.

The changes I've seen in my daughter are not natural, but I believe are based on demonic influences in her life. Once she rejected Christ, she opened herself to the influences of demonic forces. I'm not saying she's possessed, but that she's now influenced by the forces of this earth which are influenced by Satan.

So, let's look at this from a biblical perspective.

Joshua 24:15

And if it seems evil to you to serve the Lord, choose
for yourselves this day whom you will serve,
whether the gods which your fathers served
that *were* on the other side of the River, or the gods
of the Amorites, in whose land you dwell. But as for
me and my house, we will serve the Lord."

It is time to choose who we will serve, it is time to
know the Lord, and it is time to proclaim His good
news of salvation to a lost and dying world. Before
telling the Pharisees that they were children of the
devil, Jesus first told them the one thing we must be
sure of.

John 8:42

[42] Jesus said to them, "If God were your Father, you
would love Me, for I proceeded forth and came
from God; nor have I come of Myself, but He sent
Me.

We must be sure we first understand that God the
Father sent Jesus, and truly love, and know Him, as
our Lord and Savior. Let's praise His holy name.

Proverbs 30:12

There is a generation *that is* pure in its own eyes, *Yet* is not washed from its filthiness.

The Only Way

I've been working on this book for nearly three years now, although short in size I pray the content will glorify the Lord. As I've mentioned on several occasions, I've stopped many times, and started wondering if this is the right direction for me and my family. I've doubted that this was the Lord's leading, and at times I have refused to continue, questioning the Lord, but I just couldn't ignore the Lord's leading any longer.

There are many things I've realized, as I've seen the world around me change, and adopt the LGBT message, we are in a very real spiritual battle. I've also realized that not everyone caught up in the same sex lifestyle are radical, so while I don't want to paint them all with the same brush stroke, I do believe they are all lost and in need of salvation. It is the radical agenda that has been the most influential in delivering the message that their lifestyle is not sin. The Christian community, must make a stand in sharing God's truth. Ignoring the message of the evil being shoved down our throats is not an option.

I've heard, and seen, many Christian and non-Christian families that have been impacted by the desires of sexual sin. In particular, I've seen parents grieving, with few, or no outlets, for expressing their grief and pain. The worst part is that some have lost hope, and accepted this as the new normal. The only consolation I can give is that I know my hope doesn't come from the world, or what I see, or perceive, but from the Lord, and I pray that would be your hope and consolation.

In reflecting on the question that my wife and I were asked many years ago, "If we were to die today, did we know whether we were going to heaven or hell," we had no answer. In our current culture there are many that believe, or say, they would go to heaven. The question that follows naturally would be, "Why do you believe you will go to heaven?" The primary answer given usually is that, "I'm a good person." Most of us believe that we are good enough to enter heaven, but scripture does not support that thinking.

The first thing to remember is that scripture tells us there is only one way to salvation and eternal life.

John 3:16
16 For God so loved the world that He gave His only begotten Son, that whoever believes in Him should not perish but have everlasting life.

Belief in Jesus is the only way, and that leads to a person's rebirth, born again, in Christ.

John 3:3
Jesus answered and said to him, "Most assuredly, I say to you, unless one is born again, he cannot see the kingdom of God."

John 3:5

Jesus answered, "Most assuredly, I say to you, unless one is born of water and the Spirit, he cannot enter the kingdom of God.

The next thing to remember is that only those that do the will of God will enter the kingdom of heaven.

Matthew 7:21

"Not everyone who says to Me, 'Lord, Lord,' shall enter the kingdom of heaven, but he who does the will of My Father in heaven.

The beauty of it all is that you can do nothing to earn or deserve it. It is a gift from the Lord, our God and must be received in faith.

Ephesians 2:8

For by grace you have been saved through faith, and that not of yourselves; *it is* the gift of God

The Lord has given me a vision for a prayer ministry. That vision is to do exactly what He expects each of us to do, which is to pray in His full armor, for those we love, and make a stand. Even if we never see the change, or live to see it happen, there is no reason to ever believe that the Lord can't work in the lives of those we love.

I'm developing a website for a prayer ministry where I'd like to pray for those lost in sexual sin. If you are interested in joining me in prayer, please write to me at ctorres1954@outlook.com, and I'll send you information and the link to the site where I'll be outlining the details for the ministry.

I've also realized that there may be some people that are struggling with same sex attractions, or sexual desires, that they can't handle alone. If so, I'd also like to hear from you as well. I will not share any information, but will pray for those needs as well.

I'm calling on every Christian to join me in prayer, even if you don't have a family member in this lifestyle. I'm expecting the Lord to work mightily in this effort and look forward to what the Lord will do. Please pray for me, as I undertake this calling on my life.

Holy is the Lord, and worthy of our praise, His love endures forever!

www.ingramcontent.com/pod-product-compliance
Lightning Source LLC
Chambersburg PA
CBHW072011040426
42447CB00009B/1579